LEADERSHIP
ESSENTIALS

How to Lead with Passion, Pride and Purpose

Dave Mauren
Seton Hall
2016

LEADERSHIP ESSENTIALS

How to Lead with Passion, Pride and Purpose

By

Lieutenant Colonel
David S. Maurer
USA, RETIRED

With:

Komlan Joel Adzeh, Ph.D.
Joseph L. Almond
Celia K. Fayden
Paul E. Greasley, Ph.D.
Malcolm O. Munro
Lisa G. Phillips, SPHR
Jeremy R. Stinson

Main Line Press . Vanleer, TN

Leadership Essentials

How to Lead with Passion, Pride, and Purpose

ISBN: 978-0-9895795-4-4

Printed in the United States of America

Cover Layout
By
Michael Cartwright
mcartwright@comcast.net

For
Our Families, Friends, Colleagues, Teachers,
Students, and Mentors…

…and all those who attend and participate in our
seminars and workshops!

Table of Contents

Foreword

"Leadership"

It's one of the hardest words to define. Some use it as a title, others as behavior. It's a noun and a verb, a cause and an effect. *Leadership* is seen as the princess compared to its evil step-sister *Management.* Everyone seems to want it but most agree it's in short supply. We want it from our boss but get edicts instead. We expect it from our government and get dysfunction instead. We try to provide it but get pushback instead.

Does it even exist?

YES!

Six months ago, I asked several colleagues if they would be willing to share their perspectives on leadership. I had no shortage of takers. The information in this book comes from a wide range of perspectives and backgrounds and has been tested in the real world.

As a coalition of management and organizational development experts, we've spent our lives coaching and consulting with managers in all types and sizes of organizations. Our lessons learned and lessons taught are the focus of this book. We believe that leadership is a sacred practice and, properly done, results in the greatest level of efficiency.

In this compilation of essays you'll learn:

- How to get results through people
- The importance of honor
- Characteristics that define a leader
- The power of timeliness
- 20 strategies for success

- The roots and legacy of leaders today
- The importance of teaming with your HR Department
- The power of self-leadership

Who are the Authors?

This book is essentially a "Greatest Hits Collection" of some of the brightest and most experienced leadership experts I know.

Komlan Joel Adzeh, PhD.
An international scholar with expertise in organizational management.

Joseph L. Almond
A consultant with expertise in diversity and inclusion leadership and transformation.

Celia K. Fayden
A business executive with a passion for developing people.

Paul E. Greasley, Ph.D.
A fomer engineering (yes, engineering!) manager with a keen research interest in the diverse personality characteristics of servant leaders.

Dave Maurer, PMP
A retired Army officer who combines a passion for leadership development with a strong background in project management.

Lisa G. Phillips, SPHR
An HR executive who has seen first hand the importance of developing leaders in organizations.

Jeremy R. Stinson
A writer, speaker, and lifelong student and teacher of leadership.

It's been an incredible experience connecting with these experts and having them combine their experience into a great resource for those who wish to lead.

Leadership development is a journey. I hope you'll use this book as your roadmap to get the most out of your people and develop the knowledge and skills to be an awesome leader!

Towards your Total Career Success,

Malcolm O. Munro
Hired Guns Consulting, LLC

Chapter 1

Discovering Your Results-Driven Leadership Styles

By

Komlan Joel Adzeh, PhD

If we learn how to do something, we have the capability to perform in a new way. For value to occur, we have to change our behavior and use the new capability in performance. Further, our performance must be aimed at worthwhile results.

— *Robert Brinkerhoff and Stephen Gill*

A well-defined leadership role is crucial to the success of every organization. The Center of Leadership and Ethics at Duke University conducted a survey in 2009 that concluded leaderships skills positively correlated to employee performance.[i] Over the past 20 years, many organizations have conducted equally rigorous studies and ascertained that leadership strongly influenced employee performance. Peter Drucker, characterized as "the greatest management thinker of the last century" by Jack Welch, former chairman of General Electric Company, simply stated: "Leadership is all about results.[ii]"

A growing number of companies recognize the value of structuring their operations around small teams directed by formally appointed leaders. This management approach facilitates the translation of corporate visions into both behaviors and measurable outcomes. Nonetheless, these companies face difficulty in finding a way to link leadership qualities to a successful strategy that directly impacts bottom lines. This chapter is dedicated to providing leaders with techniques that will improve teams' ability to successfully achieve project goals.

Leaders across the globe are experiencing the gradual expansion of their roles, and remain under pressure to achieve (and/or exceed) goals with decreasing access to adequate resources. When the end-results are not positive indicators of the level of effort required to achieve specific leadership tasks, most self-reflect and wonder what else may be done to improve up a specific leadership technique. Bob Kings, a customer service representative in a nationally-known telecommunications firm, has first-hand experience of the angst associated to his new "leadership" assignment.

Senior management had identified Bob as an up-and-coming leader. Bob was recognized for his tenacity in accomplishing assignments, and other natural leadership qualities. He had earned a positive reputation among his peers and was respected for his self-confidence, ability to engage with customers, and to complete tasks. After a few weeks of training, Bob's enthusiasm favorably affected everyone on the project team. They were "fired up" and ready to go. From the onset of the project, Bob's management approach was clear. He sought to attain each of the milestones in sequential progression, which would lead to the larger project goals. However, much to Bob's chagrin, the results of the first performance report were disappointing. The results indicated a disconnect between Bob's leadership style and his teammates' ability to fully comprehend what was expected from them. The majority of team members struggled to adapt to Bob's management approach. Bob began to self-reflect and wonder if the performance deficiency lay in his leadership skills or the abilities of his teammates. He was tempted to shift blame to the team. Later, Bob came to realize that he was as much responsible as any team member. He needed to learn how to link his leadership qualities to the desired outcomes in order to fix the team's performance problems.

In a moment of clarity, Bob learned this essential truth: leadership is what you make out of it. The term "leadership" may convey different meanings to different people in different situations. Leaders are "special" individuals, the masterminds behind policy and the strategic orientation of an organization. Leaders have character, inspire confidence, and exude authority. Leaders are also "ordinary" employees who are committed to completing daily tasks. A leader's actions may go unnoticed, but leaders are the driving force behind an organizational success. Leaders come in every form and shape and arise when least expected. When it comes to results-driven leaders, not only do they embody the mission and values of their organizations, they also have the ability to transform these values into specific results for all the stakeholders–customers, employees, shareholders, and the public.–

Developing results-driven leaders requires a broad-minded individual with a high sense of accountability who assumes personal responsibility for the team's productivity, and ensures that each team member performs (1) in a role where an individual's skills are best maximized, and (2) the collective contributions of all team members achieve the larger project goals. It should be clear from the project kickoff that the motivation is to support the team and not to obtain a personal or political gain. Mark Wyong was clear about his motivation starting a new job as the general manager of a car dealership: "I am here to serve you, so you can better serve our customers." As Mark progressed in his career, it was the conscious alignment of his passion for sales with achieving results that inspired his employees. Mark is a perfect example of a leader's ability to motivate teammates, and successfully meet (and exceed) expectations that are critical to sustaining organizational competitiveness.

One important aspect of the results-driving leadership is long-term problem solving. Leaders are required to remove roadblocks and make the tough decisions[iii] about resource allocation, staffing, budget changes etc. While it may be easy to shift blame when a project is behind schedule or not achieving interim milestones, true leaders take full responsibility for any shortfall in team performance. They also hold accountable team members who do not perform to the expected levels of proficiency. Above all, results-driven leaders remain true to their passion of supporting their team members to achieve the fullest of their potentials. Harlan Cleveland, an American diplomat, educator, and author said: "Leaders are problem solvers by talent and temperament, and by choice." The rest of this chapter presents the Path-Goal Leadership Model as a valuable technique that utilizes leadership qualities to achieve desired outcomes.

The Background of the Path-Goal Leadership Model

Martin G. Evans initially developed the Path-Goal theory of leadership in 1970. Robert J. House, the founder of the Global Leadership and Organizational Behavior Effectiveness (GLOBE)[iv], later modified it. Robert House's approach is based on finding the right leadership style that best fits the employee and his/her work environment. In essence, this model suggests that there is a "path" that leads to every goal, and the leader must determine how it applies to each employee. Once the leader identifies the appropriate "path", he commits himself to the success of every employee. What matters most is attaining the larger project goals while ensuring team members are on the right track to hit each milestone.

The Path-Goal leadership theory is an extension of contingency theory, which was developed between the 1960s and 1970s, and also builds on two well-known motivation theories: 1) goal-setting and 2) expectancy. First, the goal-setting theory suggests that the effective way to motivate employees is setting challenging goals and recognizing achievements. Second, the expectancy theory suggests that employees will behave in a certain way if they expect that their behaviors will lead to a certain outcome, and such outcome will be meaningfully rewarded.

Problems facing organizations are complex, and they cannot be fixed by waving a magic wand. Some leaders seeking a quick fix to job performance issues may wonder why theories are important. Theories are important because they inform the practice. With the practice, people learn how to do something. But with the theory, they understand the reason why they are doing it. Theories also create the framework to make an assumption (or envision possible scenarios), particularly when people face with uncertainty and complexity. An assumption is the reflection of what is perceived to be reality. It is the meaning given to a situation, which predisposes certain behaviors. Path-Goal Leadership Model makes the assumption that team members will achieve great performance when provided with a clear path guiding their efforts.

The Path-Goal Leadership Model is practical, straightforward, and offers a structure to achieve the milestones and larger project goals. The Path-Goal Leadership Model focuses on the relationship between a formally appointed leader and his/her team members. This model characterizes what a leader needs to do rather than who he or she needs to be in order to succeed. Of course, both aspects are equally important to leadership effectiveness. Nonetheless, leaders increase their credibility and influence by producing tangible results.

Results-driven leaders use the Path-Goal Leadership Model to focus their energy on developing the skill sets of their team members and ensure operations run efficiently, and those strategies are executed decisively.

Steve Jobs, co-founder of Apple Inc., taught a lesson when he completely turned around the company, which was on the verge of bankruptcy. Jobs focused on (1) simplifying Apple's product offerings into four main quadrants, i.e., desktop and portable versions of all products, and a consumer and pro variant of each product. He succeeded even further by stoking the market's anticipation on an annual basis with his "one more thing...." addendum to each Worldwide Developers Conference, where he launched incredibly innovative and iconic products, including iMacs, iPods, iPhones, iPads, iTunes, Apple TV, and iCloud. Jobs' leadership restored the reputation of Apple and increased the company's stock price from $6 EPS to $300 EPS before he resigned in August 2011, two months before he died.[v]

More than ever before, leadership is about getting results. The business objectives of improving operational efficiency and maximizing employee potentials are the lifeblood of results-driven leadership. Such leaders ask whether team members possess the adequate skills, have the appropriate resources, and are motivated to successfully complete their individually assigned tasks. Whenever the answer to one of these questions is "no," results-driven leaders attune their styles to solve the problems. On your leadership journey, you may find the Path-Goal Leadership Model useful to remain focused on delivering outstanding results.

How to Use the Path-Goal Leadership Model

House (1996) found that a Path-Goal leader exhibits a number of behaviors (or styles) that have the potential under certain conditions to motivate team members to achieve effective performance. They include:

a. Clarifying subordinate performance goals

b. Clarifying means by which subordinates can effectively carry out tasks

c. Clarifying standards by which subordinate's performance will be judged

d. Clarifying expectancies that others hold for subordinates to which subordinates should or should not respond, and

e. Judicious use of reward and punishment contingent to performance (p.336)[4].

House suggests that leaders consider two factors – employee characteristics and work environment–to successfully deploy the Path-Goal Leadership Model.

Employee Characteristics

What characterizes employees encompasses who they are, what they know, and what motivates them. For many, a key motivational factor is the level of control they want to have over their work. Some employees believe that things that happen to them are under their own control (internal locus of control). Therefore, they take responsibility for their individual behaviors to accomplish their goals. Generally, this type of employees tends to perform well when they have flexibility to organize their work. Still, others believe that external factors determine their professional outcomes, particularly, their job performance (external locus of control). Mostly, they do not take initiative to overcome obstacles. Instead, they are energized by being provided with clear instructions to follow. The difference between these two categories of employees is not always obvious. People are generally somewhere between the two extremes. However, this basic information can help leaders understand their teammates better, respect them as individuals, and motivate them to attain high performance.

Work Environment

Effective leaders create the environment that supports their leadership initiatives. They pay attention to the job structures, the authority system, and the team dynamics. Your employees expect that you are familiar with the setting of their work and the daily challenges they face. They also expect leaders to use their authority wisely. For the tasks that are complex, team members expect the leader to provide a clear guidance for job performance. Some tasks require a team-work, and involve lots of interactions among team members. Team dynamics refers to the extent to which employees maintain a good working relationship with one another, collaborate together, and support one another. The results-driven leader should foster team members' commitment to achieve common goals.

The Path-Goal Leadership Model suggests that employees are motivated to perform better when individual and environmental needs are met. Therefore, the results-driven leaders should adapt their styles to the situation they face, e.g., the personality and the motivation preferences of their team members in order to achieve the best result. The figure on the next page summarizes the Path-Goal Leadership Model.

Path-Goal Leadership Model		
Employee Characteristics	**Motivation Preferences**	**Leader's Responses**
External Locus of Control	Trust Recognition	Achievement-Oriented Leadership
	Clarity Guidance	Directive leadership
Internal Locus of Control	Inclusion Collaboration	Participative Leadership
	Empathy Consideration	Supportive Leadership

There are four leadership styles associated with the Path-Goal Leadership Model. They represent neither personal traits nor intrinsic characteristics of a leader. Instead, they are behaviors that a leader adopts and adapts to the needs of team members. These styles emphasize what leaders do, rather than who they are or should be. Therefore, a single leader may embody a distinct style or a combination of the four styles as the circumstance requires.

Achievement-oriented Leadership

An achievement-oriented leadership style involves setting challenging goals for your team. A results-driven leader trusts the capacity of the team member to attain set milestones and excel. This leader emphasizes continuous improvement and rewards exceptional achievements. This type of leadership is effective with team members who are experts in their fields, have external locus of control, and are motivated by formal authority, which dictates simple and structured tasks. Savvy leaders, with this information, take their teams to new heights by providing a flexible work arrangement while incrementally raising minimum performance standards.

Directive Leadership

This leadership style ensures that employees' daily duties are very clear. Leaders practicing this leadership style should deconstruct complex processes into specific steps, and ensure all team members comprehend those steps. Team members who are motivated by directive leadership are usually self-starters, open-minded, and need minimal supervision to close tasks. However, they may need periodic reassurance that their skills are being appropriately applied. Generally, these employees have moderate job skills and external locus of control. They are driven by formal authority and excel at completing complex and ambiguous tasks. Leaders who practice directive leadership have a great responsibility to provide specific guidance at whichever level it's needed.

Participative Leadership

Many highly talented employees are energized by the participative leadership style. They have internal locus of control and want to be included in the decision making. They may be comfortable with either strong or weak formal authority. They easily adjust to complex or ambiguous tasks. These team members value collaboration, and results-driven leaders are not expected to dictate rules for them to follow. Leaders must consult on regular basis with this type of team members to ensure that effective knowledge transfer occurs. Constantly taking this approach will provide the requisite motivation for extra effort to achieve great performance.

Supportive Leadership

Supportive leadership is slightly different from participative leadership. Supportive leadership requires the results-driven leader to ensure team members are aware of leadership's full support and that higher value is placed on individual success over the leader's own success. This type of team member requires constructive feedback to create opportunities for growth and professional development. The results-driven leader must treat this type of team member with respect and express concern for both their individual well-being and their need for a work-life balance. Flexibility is the new norm for employee commitment. When both parties negotiate the trade-offs fairly, flexibility is a powerful source of motivation.

Peter Benissan worked for Mark Wyong. He prided himself of being a top performer at work. While in graduate school, Peter registered for a course that met on campus on Saturdays from 9:00am until 12:00pm. Saturday was his office's busiest day of the week, and he could not afford to be away too long. However, once he proved to his manager that he could meet the expectation while working for only one-half day on Saturday, his manager allowed him this flexibility in schedule. Peter exceeded all expectations during that period and put his team on the top.[vi] Employees who are inspired by the supportive leadership style have high skills and internal locus of control. They thrive in simple, structured, and friendly work environments. They are energized when consideration is shown for their external needs.

Most may not have control over the way jobs are structured or how team members are selected; however, your understanding of the Path-Goal leadership styles may be an invaluable step to improving your team performance. The leader who sets proper expectations for the amount and quality of work to be produced– while recognizing that each team member is unique– has a profound influence on productivity. Bob in the earlier example (or any professional in a quest for a results-driven leadership), will likely benefit from the Path-Goal Leadership Model.

Experienced leaders know that a perfect team doesn't exist. However, when a particular situation warrants the application of a specific or a combination of Path-Goal leadership techniques, you don't want to be cut off guard. While some leaders may be limited in the changes they can make, the results-driven leaders will find that they can bring a real value to their organizations through the Path-Goal Leadership Model. You may begin this journey by engaging your team members. Next, you should examine what might constitute obstacles to achieve great performance and provide the appropriate remedies.

As leaders are trying to adjust to the changing work environment and the increasing expansion of their roles, they recognize that there is no one-size-fits-all way to improve job performance. Therefore, they seek to develop a wide-range of skills to meet the needs of their organizations. The merit of the Path-Goal Leadership Model is that it bridges the divide between who the leader is and what he actually accomplishes. At the time when job performance has become the best measurement of leadership effectiveness, the results-driven leadership styles challenge leaders to be proactive and to foster an atmosphere where employees believe that their leaders are genuinely committed to their success. Occasional shortfalls should not be seen as a failure but as a learning experience. Successful leaders inspire by the support they provide. They justify their authority by the results they obtain.

About the Author

Komlan Joel Adzeh is a Business Strategist and International Management Consultant. His passion is to see managers and employees overcome the natural obstacles to success, and reach their full potential. His mission is to partner with leaders and assist them in developing a committed workforce that understands their vision and successfully carries out their mission.

He is a co-author of *The Big Book of Management. Tools and Techniques Every Manager Needs in their Toolbox.* He is also a qualified facilitator of personality, career, and organizational development assessments such as Myers-Briggs Type Indicator®, Strong, CPI™, and FIRO®.

His business strategy background includes substantial experience in retail industry, both domestic and international. He is fluent in French, and He has led contract negotiations with a number of corporations in Europe and Africa.

Following more than a decade of expertise in creating value for customers, he understands the daunting challenges that many managers and business leaders face. He has a unique insight on issues related to organization management. With his wide-ranging experience, he is a trusted partner to enhance the capability of any organization.

He holds a Bachelor and a Masters in Business Management, MBA in Government Acquisition, and a Doctorate in Organization and Management.

To contact him, please visit *www.komlanjoeladzeh.com* or email: *drjoelconsulting@gmail.com*

Chapter 2

Honor is Honor

By

Joseph L. Almond

"All the great things are simple, and many can be expressed in a single word: freedom, justice, honor, duty, mercy, hope."

– Winston Churchill

I believe honor is a very important quality for a leader to demonstrate. I read that honor is the courage to do what is right, no matter what. It's a belief that your actions represent more than just yourself, the recognition that what you do defines your entire generation. It's not enough to do what is acceptable to others but more important to do what's acceptable to yourself. Some will say that this notion is subjective. Basically thinking that some believe in honor and others don't. I submit we all know what honor is and our level of submission to it is what's open to subjectivity. We all know what's right and wrong and at the end of the day we make our choices. With those choices come consequences some we can live with others we can't.

Leaders that understand and embrace honor are the leaders that have others that will follow them anywhere. Honor seems to be a lost art and science. It's something read about however not something that is always embraced. I recently facilitated a class and I was sharing a book that was originally written in 1989 and the suggestion was that the concept was dated. This book has sold over twenty-five million copies. For me this was very interesting because I know that honor is very important to this organization. What was great is that as I pondered what was said I realized that honor can never be dated. The truth is the truth and will stand the test of time. Honor is honor and never goes out of style. It has always been welcomed, accepted or rejected. It's never been a fad, or the soup of the day. It's real and employees are looking for it consciously and subconsciously in their leaders. It's unfortunate that honor is considered dated among some leaders and employees alike. It's unfortunate that what seems to be the norm is actually not the norm. Dishonorable leadership is excused and in some cases rewarded. We accept it as OK and make excuses for it. When did we allow honor to be the exception and not the rule? It's amazing how the standard of what's acceptable has changed and become the status quo. I began this chapter mentioning that honor is doing what right no matter what. This a tall order to fill especially the more power a leader has. However, that doesn't give a leader a pass. I submit the more power the more responsibility. For much is given for much is required. Choosing honor should be an automatic decision; it's the courage to do what is right, no matter what. A belief that your actions represent more than just yourself, the recognition that what you do defines your entire generation should be forethought actually it should be an automatic thought.

One of the finest leaders I ever had the pleasure of knowing was a soldier. She was my commanding officer when I first became a noncommissioned officer. I watched her style of leadership and patterned some of my leadership after her. She is a WestPoint graduate and exemplifies honor in her service. For her leadership is built on the foundation of honor. I was a very young soldier and prior to serving under her I had not experienced a leader with such great honor. She is a woman of her word and always put the needs of the soldiers she led as a top priority. I remember beginning my career as a leader and thinking I want to be this type of leader. She gave our unit tremendous goals to accomplishing while providing us with the tools needed to accomplish those goals. We all knew she would give us the truth about situations we would encounter and the support needed to excel. She ensured her leadership team understood and accepted and adopted honorable leadership as our way of being. She developed the character of those who served with her. She emphasized not just what we were as soldiers; but also our character as men and women, husbands, wives, daughters and sons. The character development with honor as the driving force has stayed with me my entire career. My commanding officer led with honor and set the expectation and held me accountable to a standard of honor. I will forever be grateful for this. I have been fortunate to work with numerous organizations over the past two decades. I truly enjoy learning from great leaders directly and indirectly. The honorable leaders I have worked with were willing to do whatever it takes to make decisions of integrity and treat people with respect and dignity. They took pride in holding on to their character and values at all costs. Some of their decisions were met with extreme opposition from those who would have preferred for them to compromise their honor and self-respect. These leaders are unapologetic and uncompromising about their beliefs. The result of their honor is employees who can trust that their leader will do the right thing at all costs especially when no one is looking. This creates greater synergy and a morally and ethically environment that is capable of greatness. This creates an organizational culture that is second to none. This leader leads not with just inspiring words but more so with inspiring deeds. They walk the walk which is more impactful than the talk alone. The alignment of leading with honor and not just talking about it is imperative. Organizations around the globe are looking for the best and brightest talent they can find. However, those that can deliver on their talents and skills with honor and distinction will survive the test of time.

"The most tragic thing in the world is a man of genius who is not a man of honor."

– George Bernard Shaw

I recently watched an episode of one of my favorite television shows. Two colleagues who'd worked together for thirty years were talking. One who is the head of the organization had recently found out his friend had been falsifying reports leading everyone to believe he was doing a much better job in his department then he was. The leader of the organization is a very honorable leader and that is his legacy. He told his old friend "All you have is your word, and when you don't have your word, you don't have life"

"Mine honor is my life; both grow in one; Take honor from me, and my life is done."

– William Shakespeare

I found this to be very simple yet very profound. The other gentlemen was seeking a promotion because of financial problems and was willing to cheat and dishonor a stellar career to get ahead. Not only did the leader of the organization not promote his friend but he also told him he would be demoted or he could resign based on his actions. The gentleman dishonored himself as well as the organization for personal financial gain. His leader demonstrated honor in how he handled the situation. He didn't allow thirty years of friendship to stand in the way of doing the right thing.

"Rather fail with honor than succeed by fraud."

- Sophocles

Recently I looked at my military Honorable Discharge certificate. I seldom look at it however, I realized for the first time in over 20 years the significance of what the certificate represents. I made decisions and demonstrated honorable actions decades ago that afforded me great opportunity then and into my future. I also realize my honorable service has and will impact the lives of my children and grandchildren. There are privileges that come with honorable service to veterans and their families. I am grateful to know the value of honor and its lasting impact.

"Nobody can acquire honor by doing what is wrong."

– Thomas Jefferson

I believe it's a choice whether to be honorable or not. Leader sometimes blame a lack of honor on their boss or their employees or the organizational culture. I submit leaders need to lead and stand up and be the example of honor for their employee's and organizations. They must stand up even if they are standing alone. Honor needs to be the rule and not the exception. Honor is not some sacred character trait of the early periods of the world. If there was ever a time for leaders to demonstrate honor the time is now. History has given us numerous stories of honorable men and women you faced adversity and did the right thing often times against all odds. What will history write about our current leaders of today?

"Who sows virtue reaps honor." – Leonardo da Vinci.

We are in a time in our society where the television, internet and radio have tremendous power and influence. However there are leaders driving these mediums. Imagine more honorable expressions being publicized and emphasized. Some would say that could impact their success in a negative manner. I submit that the honorable leader can lead others to greater heights and successes. Honor is honor.

"Success without honor is an unseasoned dish; it will satisfy your hunger, but it won't taste good." *- Joe Paterno*

About Joseph L. Almond:

Joseph Almond is an Army veteran, author, speaker and coach. He holds a Masters of Arts Degree in Organizational Leadership. He provides customized keynotes, coaching and training programs. His expertise in diversity and inclusion leadership and transformation has assisted numerous organizations.

Joseph brings his experience with government, schools, non-profit, and business to his presentations. He captures imaginations while stimulating the intellect. Since professional life is an extension of a person's personal life he incorporates relevant life experiences in a compelling way to connect deeply with his audiences.

He has over 20 years of professional speaking experience. He is the author of the book *Get Better Not Bitter* in which he inspires others to live their best life in the midst of adversity. He is also the co-author of *The Big Book of Management.*

Joseph's diverse career has equipped him to interface with a multitude of individuals employed in a number of progressive organizations nationally and internationally.

Chapter 3

Leadership Characteristics
By
Celia K. Fayden

When presented with the topic of leadership, my first thought was how do I write to what I believe is natural and intuitive as a business professional. What do I really know about what it is to be a leader or hold a leadership role? Do I research the topic to the point of overwhelming proportions? Is what I know enough?

Professionally, I have held many leadership roles with ever increasing responsibility throughout my career, managing projects and people, in several platforms of business. In review of my career over the years, my experiences working in many different industries from property management to education (children and adults), finance to defense contractor and even co-owner of a small database company, the common theme was the same. Treat others the way you would like to be treated and if it's real and authentic all good things will be reaped in the end, no matter the outcome.

With any of the industries that I worked with either consulting or job, I had a great deal of respect and commitment to the company and the people I worked with. It may not have always been said, as not all times are good but my commitment was always in place to do the right thing and a job well done.

So the question that kept lurking was are leaders just naturally born or are they hand-picked and groomed for leadership positioning? Does the grooming of potential leaders make them better candidates then say, Trey, who just has a natural knack for leading teams? This person who has every bit of the qualities of a leader but is overlooked? My belief is that a leader's character, good or bad is developed and cultivated by every influencing factor in their life to that particular point in time. They are born with their natural instincts and their experiences in life frame who they become, whether it be leading an organization or a leader as part of a team, sometimes being referred to as the follower, is the right place for that individual.

You are a leader from the day you are born, with innate characteristics of your "essential[vii] self" or who you are at the core. Life experiences and influences play a large part in who you become and how those influences play out as the "social self" you portray to the world. When the two are in sync, magic happens. So, where does leadership fall into all of this? We are leaders of our lives every day and we face decisions that have impact and will affect others. Whether we choose to take the role in which we lead a team to a specific outcome, or are an influencer or follower, all are leaders in the role of "choice" in that project or event. Are there caveats to that comment? Of course, so the focus here is how leadership and the leader role apply to our professional career and experiences. If we are born leaders, how will we define and grow our leadership skills beyond the wall of expectation? What is really important to you as a leader? Is it to be out front on center stage or is the supporting roll what drives our success? You decide.

How Does Leadership and the Leader Role Apply to our Professional Career?

In reminiscing on experiences of leadership and how it impacts teams and professional careers, the story of mother comes to mind, her children attending a public school considered a bit out of the norm. It was called the public school with a "private school" twist. The parents had direction and say about the content, books and culture of the school. It was a collaborative environment where parents, administration and teachers worked together for the common good of the children. The school used a different methodology to reading called Spalding[viii] which was used to guide children in developing their reading skills. I was the young mother who had a growing interest in what this Spalding method was all about and how that would be translated to my children. Through many questions and curiosity, I found a protégé who knew and worked directly with Ms. Spalding. She happened to be the new principle of the school, she provided guidance and understanding of the philosophy. I too, could study and learn the Spalding methodology. It was important to understand what my children would learn, as I would be responsible to work with them at home and if I didn't get it how could I help them, so I signed up for a course. At the time it was quite unusual for a parent to be interested in this sort of program at the certification level, but I was really interested and the education came to benefit me later on.

After completing the certification, I felt compelled to take that knowledge back to the school. Many new students coming into the school did not have the foundation of Spalding and yet it was a requirement of understanding in all grade levels. So I used that instruction at the school by establishing a before short school session for new students coming. Over time, we leveraged a handful of parents very familiar with the Spalding method to provide transition for those students coming in from first grade to eighth grade and to those students that had need for tutoring. It was a great joy for me to work with such amazing students, parents, teachers and administration. An overwhelming success for everyone!

How We Define and Grow our Leadership Skills?

My leadership style comes with heart and understanding of what it takes to lead high performing teams. Everyone's style is different and no one style is right but there is certain knowledge and characteristics of a good leader which are intuitive but also can be learned and developed. I remember a conversation a long ago with one of my colleagues. This person had implied on several occasions that I am not demanding enough to be a leader. In clarification, she thought leaders should be demanding, forceful and arrogant, that someone who treated others well was a weakness.

I see leadership as several pieces of a bigger picture, whether it be leading an organization or running teams on smaller projects.

Listening to Learn	Talk less and listen more, keep an open mind to the possibilities for creativity, improvement and change
Enthusiasm	A positive attitude is an attitude for greatness. It contagious and makes even the most gloomy of circumstances seem a little brighter

Accountability	The old adage of saying what you will do and doing what you say; being approachable and understanding mistakes, they happen and we learn nothing if it all comes out perfect every time
Develop the Team	Understand that their success is your success. Provide the team with training and resources to do their jobs, listen to your team and be responsive. Disciplined yet flexible.
Expectations	Set clear expectations, scope, schedule and budget. Work collaboratively with the team for clear understanding through all streams of communication. In person, phone, email, one on one or as groups. As a leader understand the team and how they best communicate. Execute by keeping the end goal in mind.
Respect	It is very important to respect all cultural boundaries, which takes some education and building of relationships. Appreciating work / life balance. It comes back to treating others the way you wish to be treated.
Scheduling Points	Acknowledge the timelines when events or activities need to be completed. The mantra of "Trust, then verify" is good. Pulse those in the team that are accountable to a timeline. Provide open dialogue if the timelines are or are not appropriate to close. As a leader, provide opportunity for comfortable dialogue and resource support. Again set the expectation on both sides.

Humility	Everyone should have the opportunity to be a contributor. There is no "I" in TEAM[ix]. Collaboration and teams working together are the game changer.
Integrity and Loyalty	Integrity is your backbone. Do the right thing for yourself and others. Leading a team is also leading by example with the right heart.
Passion	Create the environment that is conducive to growth and opportunity. If a person is in a position that is just not right for them, help them seek their real calling. Inspire professional and personal excellence to build confidence, trust and pride.

"Trust, then verify", is good, not as a micromanager but rather with active participation, open discussion with individuals on the team for status and any requirements that need to be worked. If there is a need for clarification, consult or any other aspect of responsibility, conversations continue to take place so pulse checks are important with the accountable person on point to status, that person is the lead in their own right.

It is often said to be successful you need to surround yourself with the best talent. Agreed, it needs to be diverse and the right talent for the specific project. Nothing wrong with that except when you can't obtain "that" person in whatever situation. On those occasions, spin it right to create an opportunity for someone in the organization; building bench strength, new growth, and a stretch assignment for the volunteer point person via a mentor and some training.

Case in point, recently we added someone to our writing team for a new project. He had never written to this topic, much less a proposal. Our expert was going on maternity soon and had lots on her plate as well. We determined the best approach would be for her to sit down with him in a 2-day session, outline and discuss the overall project, lay out the requirements, schedule meeting times for them to get back together and revisit the status of the writing project at those times. Additionally, if he had any questions along the way, he was encouraged to call on this mentor for guidance as needed. It was very successful and a win win situation for the team. This new write building his skill set for greater value to himself and also for the company. His mentor had bench strength for when she would leave for maternity calling. Looking for opportunities to grow talent on teams, you can't do any better than that. Always seeking a back-up plan.

Leading teams and being a leader is about creating a positive environment even when the uncomfortable happens and it does happen. Take accountability without any smoke and mirrors, just clarity of what is real, successes and mistakes will happen, regardless. Have a focus on the goal, work a schedule that is reasonable, which is sometimes VERY difficult to do. Set expectations and communicate, if your team does not sense they can come to you to discuss their challenges whether it be delegation, lack of resource, information or understanding, there will be an issue. As a leader accountability and support are key to your success. Another quote, I have said often is "You are only as successful as your team, so their success will be your success." If you don't feed your team, it only reflects on you and beating them down will only light a fire where you don't want one to be.

Build and nurture the right culture for your teams. Culture in the organization is top down and filters everywhere. It is often misunderstood, but is very important. I mentioned earlier that there was not one organization that I had worked for that I did not have a great deal of respect for. Each of the companies had respect in their industry among their peers and customers. Several years ago, I worked with a software application training company, Training a la Carte (TALC), it was created by two woman who had a vision and to this day I have a great admiration to what these wonderful ladies did and the opportunity they provided to me. I was just getting back into the workforce, stay at home engineer, raising two young boys when I was called by a peer asking if I would like to go back to work part-time. I was to interview with Janet and Fran, which out of sheer fear I put off doing for several months. When I finally went in for my second interview with them, it was to be a demo of my training abilities. Fran and Janet were both totally different people, Fran, quiet and shrewd business professional and Janet, lively with great people skills and both strong technical expertise in their own applications. In the training demo, Janet knew the application and made some craziness on the screen and asked how I might fix it. I looked at the monitor and had no clue, which was quite obvious with my jaw hanging wide open. I looked at them both and just said, "We will have a break shortly, I will explore what has occurred and we can address it after the break with the class", thinking it could be made into a teaching moment… for me…

Janet told me something I did not expect. She said, "I can teach you technical all day long, I can't teach you integrity, thank you." I had sold both of them on that last moment. These two ladies sold me on the culture they wanted to instill not only for all those that came to work for them and Training a la Carte but for their customers as well. That was the beginning to a long, rewarding working relationship that lasted more than 15 years.

During that time, a friend of mine share a most intriguing book. The "Customer Comes Second", by Hal F. Rosenbluth[x], a very interesting title for someone who was always told and therefore believed that the customer was right and was always first to a growing business. After reading this book, my perspective was wavering on my original knowledge. So I began practicing the concepts in my teams. What I found is there was merit to the idea that when you enlighten, communicate, mentor, and develop your staff, they feel valued and acknowledged. The rewards can be exponential.

Through effective leadership a team will perform to the highest standards and reciprocally they treat their customers better resulting in more business, loyal employees and ultimately, customers which generates more revenue and profits.

So what is REALLY important as a Leader?

A culmination of characteristics of the whole person. It is a two-way street but if I were to list three things that are at the top of my leader board, they would be:

1. **TRUST, HONESTY AND INTEGRITY.** Everyone wants to work with a trustworthy individual that will lead the team to a successful conclusion. In reality that is not always the case. As leaders, it is important to establish your role up front. If something is new and different, as was encouraged earlier on in the chapter, there will also be failures and mistakes. Credibility will be shaken if there is no accountability for mistakes or failure. Trust is built on leadership response and proactivity to circumstances gone astray.

2. **COMPETENCE.** Just saying you're competent at being a leader, but more important at demonstrating it with past achievements and acknowledgements. If you as a leader have honors in your back pocket, let them shine but also recognize not to gloat and show arrogance, that comes back to the trait of humility, there is a fine line. Along that thread is intelligence which comes with a continual learning commitment. Not to say going for an advanced degree is the answer, it would depend on where you are at in life and whether it is an option. There are so many avenues to obtain credentials and grow knowledge and expertise.

3. **INSPIRATION FOR TODAY AND FUTURE.** Everyone smiles when they are truly inspired. What I have found is that an inspiring leader is great at telling stories and creating an image for his/her team of the possibilities of what can be. The whole point of leadership is for the team to know .... Where do we go from here? What are the short and long-term goals for the organization? Communicate, communicate, and communicate more. Can't get better than that. This provides confidence in the organization and an understanding for the future. In going back to the book, the Customer Comes Second, I had read that due to the business landscape, layoffs were eminent. However it did not deter the employees. Because of their mantra and how their employees felt valued, many had opted to take a cut in pay rather than lose their jobs. Once business perked up, salaries were restored, now that is inspiring and forward thinking!

About Celia Fayden

Ms. Fayden enjoys a successful career as a business development management professional with more than 15 years of experience in leadership and team member roles supporting the entire BD capture lifecycle in proposal management. She has acquired expert-level knowledge of strategy, competitive intelligence analysis, and business development in both the Government and commercial market spaces during her tenure as a proposal manager, program manager, and business development analyst.

Leveraging the skills and insights developed over multiple years of supporting dozens of winning captures, the direct application of Ms. Fayden's comprehensive knowledge of effective proposal management techniques adapted from capture management industry leaders like Shipley, APMP, and Lohfield Consulting, she is directly responsible for retaining existing contracts and winning several hundred million dollars' worth of new business.

Ms. Fayden's approach to customer support is holistic. She immerses herself in discussions with subject matter experts and executive leadership to understand the customer's technical challenges relative to the technical solution offered in the proposal.

Ms. Fayden demonstrates outstanding interpersonal skills, excellent communication, management and organizational skills. She is terrific in coordinating the work efforts of multi-disciplinary teams on-site or virtually. Her specialties include beginning to end proposal management, professional development, program management, coaching, team leadership, policy administration, contracts, budget and time management, and customer relationships.

Core Competencies:

Proposal Management, Effective Communications, Business Development, Active Listening, Proactive Leadership, Strategy, Competitive Intelligence, Budgetary Management, Corporate Training, Professional Development, Small Business Ownership, Managing Teams

Chapter 4

The Timely Leader:

Appreciating "Time" as a Distinguishing

Characteristic of Leadership

By

Paul E. Greasely, PhD

The following events took place many years ago but I still remember them very, very well. I was an experienced aerospace engineer and had accepted a new position with a different company as a way of enhancing my career. I joined a team of other engineers who had just started work on a new business proposal to develop an advanced helicopter propulsion system. Saturday work was the norm and I was there trying to contribute to the team while still learning the names of everyone around the conference table. Frankly, I was in over my head.

The door to the room opened and a man entered who I did not recognize but everyone stopped and acknowledged as someone of consequence. He greeted everyone and thanked them for being part of the project. He briefly explained the history behind what we were doing, its current importance, and how it would benefit many people in the future. He listened intently as the team continued its work with renewed energy.

After some time the conversation slowed down and he turned to me and said, "Paul, you're new around here. What do you think?" Incredible! He knew my name! He validated my presence as a team member and wanted my opinion! The Vice President responsible for the entire program had confidence in me and expected me to contribute to the success of the team. What a great start!

The Timely Leader

While driving home I reflected on the experience and discerned that the Vice President had used the notion of "time" as a way of communicating to the proposal team the significance of what we were doing. The past was important because it provided a basis for the present and we were ready to perform as a result of our mutual history, experience, and skill. The present was important because what we were doing was relevant and all the pieces to the puzzle were coming together at just the right moment in time. The future was important because the results of our innovative work would create a better tomorrow. Yes, at the end of the project the team was successful and we all celebrated together. And yes, the Vice President consistently appealed to the notion of time throughout his long and successful career.

Thus began my deliberate study of the "timely leader". I define a timely leader as someone who intentionally places their leadership style and organizational life in correct relationship with the revealed past and the perceived future to effectively accomplish objectives in the present. This process takes place in time with the intent to produce positive consequential change. The timely leader is skilled at making sense of the signs of the times and responding appropriately. The timely leader fully appreciates the uniqueness of words such as generation, season, hour, moment, and how different cultures uniquely perceive the passage of time.

Time matters. Hodgkinson (2001) observed that "we are always creatures of our times and the times themselves are a flood of events that are always somehow out of focus" (p. 298). Paz (1997), a Mexican Nobel Prize author and diplomat, boldly stated "I believe that the reformation of our civilization must begin with a reflection on time" (p. 24). There are at least two kinds of time. 'Chronos' is abstract, measurable, sequential, or chronological time whereas 'kairos' is the human and living time of intentions and actions. 'Chronos' can be quantitatively measured as a length or duration of time. Johnson (1997) explains that "clock time matters primarily because we use it to orient ourselves to what other people expect of us" (p. 80). Conversely, 'kairos' refers to time in the sense of the right or the most opportune time. It is a qualitative moment of undetermined chronological time when something significant happens. In this sense, "time is useful because it contributes to a sense of structure as we participate in social life" (Johnson, 1997, p. 80).

The timely leader understands both the chronos and kairos of time and the fact that it is a limited, non-renewable organizational resource. Timely leaders guide and show the way from the past, through the present, and into the future. The timely leader understands that he is a product of his own time and the times in which he lives. He can only act within his own understanding and definition of time. He has wrestled with Tennyson's observation that 'today is yesterday's tomorrow and tomorrow's yesterday'.

There are many definitions of a leader and the function of their leadership. Assuredly, we all recognize good leadership when we experience it and we struggle unnecessarily when we experience poor leadership. Everything rises and falls on the leader. Specifically, a timely leader can be characterized by:

1- a focused vision,

2- self-motivated movement, and

3- organizing the efforts of others.

This definition of a timely leader is based on Laub's (2004) general definition of a leader as a "person who sees a vision, takes action toward the vision, and mobilizes others to become partners in pursuing change" (p. 4) and leadership as an "intentional change process through which leaders and followers, joined by a shared purpose, initiate action to pursue a common vision" (p. 5). Laub's succinct yet inclusive definitions are worthy of careful consideration.

A Timely Leader has a Focused Vision

Vision suggests the ability to see something and a timely leader can see things that others cannot see. He sees a future defined by a personal vision that is focused on something different than the present. The future state is recognized as a place more desirable than the present. As a result, the present condition becomes a bit uncomfortable and even unsettling. The future focused vision is like a magnet pulling the timely leader in the direction of their vision.

A timely leader is intentional about becoming more self-aware. He has examined his fundamental values, beliefs, and assumptions about leadership and himself as a person. He has considered the source of his values, the origin of his beliefs, and is confident in his assumptions. Yet he realizes with the passage of time and the accumulation of more and more life experiences that there is an ongoing need to increase the measure of his self-awareness. He knows the tension between his commitments and being open to new ideas and realities.

The result is that the timely leader has a proper understanding of and trust in his motives, feelings, and desires. He knows his boundaries and limitations when it comes to making choices and when preparing to make tough decisions. He can look confidently to a time in the past when he made good decisions using unselfish motives, harnessed his feelings using principles of emotional intelligence, and channeled his own desires to achieve something beyond himself.

The focused vision of a timely leader is more attractive than the present situation and is worth the effort to exert energy to move toward that vision. Otherwise, the timely leader is only a dreamer and his dreams are only dreams.

A Timely Leader is Driven by Self-Motivated Movement

The focused vision of a timely leader has clarity and acts as a powerful self-motivator. The possibility of turning their vision into reality consumes their waking moments and awakens them from a sound sleep. There is a certain amount of personal risk and fear of failure in turning dreams into realities. However, the timely leader purposefully begins the task of bringing to life their focused vision using their own resources of time, skill, experience, aptitude, talent, knowledge, and when required even their money.

There is self-motivated movement to achieve something that does not exist in the present. Time begins to take on a greater value with the awareness that increasing age means decreasing time to accomplish their vision. When something is in limited supply it becomes more valuable. Time becomes a resource that must be utilized carefully. The timely leader realizes the transient nature of time and how their own appreciation of time has taken on a new significance. Priorities have been adjusted and the equation of life is rebalanced with new and ever challenging factors.

When a timely leader begins to expend their own resources the notion of "alignment" becomes important. They know they are strategically aligned or aimed in a direction that will, in time, ultimately conclude in some destination or outcome. The timely leader is intentional about knowing their objectives. They understand that they have arrived in their current state as a result of historic consequence and that present tense decision making will have future consequences. The timely leader recognizes their role as an agent of change in taking decisive, self-motivated steps over time towards achieving their personal vision.

Timely leaders learn the importance of becoming both creative and innovative. Personal creativity is demonstrated when achieving their vision requires responding to the same set of circumstances with a different outcome. The missing element emerges as a new insight or alternative solution and it makes good sense. Innovation is not the same as creativity. Creativity is personal whereas innovation involves others and their support to bring a vision to life on a broad scale. When the timely leader begins to consider the notion of innovation, they understand that their vision has become larger than themselves.

A Timely Leader Organizes the Efforts of Others

Ultimately the timely leader reaches a time when they have energized and extrapolated their own efforts to the maximum. The focused vision has emerged well and there is no more they can accomplish with their own limited personal resources. It is time to introduce the unconstrained resources of others in an organized manner that will produce the maximum beneficial results. The timely leader is now in the process of sharing their focused vision and their use of personal resources with others. The task is to build an organization that will grow strong and remain viable over time.

Leadership can be defined as an intentional influence process and the timely leader deeply understands that the relationship between a leader and a follower is based in trust. A follower has many motivations but the best motive is when the follower trusts the vision of the timely leader and it becomes a mutually shared vision of the future. This occurs through clear, consistent, and continuous communication of the vision from the timely leader to the entire organization at every level. The actions of the timely leader must be transparently reliable and dependable as trustworthy relationships are built between people and among different groups in the organization. Building trust is directly linked to building a chronology of timely events that demonstrate supportive relationships between leaders and followers.

The longer the timely leader continues to pursue a vision in concert with others, the more the organization as a whole realizes that their mutual efforts can be characterized as "service" in the sense that they are supporting each other as well as others. Service can be thought of as any value-added activity that makes things better. The timely leader understands the notion of service as intrinsic motivation to establish trustworthy relationships with others while moving towards a mutually shared vision. Followers understand the notion of service as willing support for the timely leader while being an integral part of achieving something larger than themselves. Hard work is sustained over time with a proper perspective of service.

The timely leader will always find building an organization the most demanding and time consuming characteristic of their leadership skills because of the dynamic and ever complex nature of working with others. Personalities differ, conflicts erupt, communication falters, and events in time outside the influence of the timely leader emerge periodically. Yet the timely leader perseveres with confidence in their vision of the future that remains like a magnet pulling them toward a better tomorrow. Effective systems and processes acknowledge the value of time. Efficient delegation coupled with accountability acknowledges the multiplication of effort when others are united around a time limited objective. Timely recognition of excellent performance acknowledges the importance of celebrating historical achievements. And ultimately the timely leader acknowledges their own time limited nature and succession plans are prepared to help assure that the timely effort of everyone remains long into the future.

Important Concluding Thoughts

Life is lived in the present but the present moment seems to appear and vanish much too quickly. The above description of a timely leader was presented as a very serial process with the three defining elements of their leadership style occurring distinctly one after another. Obviously time occurs in a serial, linear manner while our lived out experiences are much more chaotic. The three characteristics of a timely leader sometimes occur concurrently. Yet timely leadership is a decided mindset that works in the arena of both personal and organizational life. The timely leader has a better appreciation for the timeliness of time than their contemporaries who only understand time as the passage of hours.

When considering the notions of time past, time present, and time future; conventional wisdom suggests that the past is the easiest to understand, the present is confusing at best, and the future is impossible to know with certainty. However, in the "modern world we have reversed this wisdom - generally ignoring the importance of the past, exaggerating our knowledge of the present, and presuming to speak accurately of the future when quite simply we can't" (Guinness, 2003, p. 16). Perhaps modern organizations need more strategic historians than strategic planners. The timely leader brackets their appreciation of time to intentionally consider the full measure of time.

In conclusion, here are some thoughts to consider regarding the notion of a timely leader and their leadership:

1. Timely leadership is both a skill that can be developed and an art that can be practiced over time.

2. Timely leadership can begin at any time in the life of a leader and used to their ongoing advantage.

3. Timely leadership is temporal with both a beginning and an ending and, as a result, should be considered as a full time vocational calling.

4. Timely leadership is responsive to the fact that different cultures have a unique understanding of time and interpret time differently.

5. Timely leadership perceives the existence of time based cause and effect linkages implying that the future is in the present and can be imagined by analysis and discerning insights.

6. Timely leadership provides a unique way of considering and assessing criteria in the decision making process.

7. Timely leadership is more apt to use inferential statistical processes to bring some clarity to the emerging future based on better insights to the past and present.

8. Timely leadership enables a broader meaning to the idea of the present as a way of better understanding the past and the future.

9. Timely leadership provides a unique opportunity to cooperate with time in the passage of time past, time present, and time future.

10. Timely leadership creates a distinctive and enveloping way of looking at the concepts of vision, motivation, and organizing.

Each of these standalone thoughts offers the opportunity to consider your own ideas about a timely leader. Think well and enjoy!!

References

Guinness, O. (2003). Prophetic untimeliness: A challenge to the idol of relevance, Grand Rapids, MI: Baker Books.

Hodgkinson, C. (2001). Tomorrow, and tomorrow, and tomorrow: A post-postmodern purview, International Journal of Leadership in Education, 4(4), 297-307.

Johnson, A. G. (1997). The forest and the trees: Sociology as life, practice, and promise. Philadelphia, PA: Temple University Press.

Laub, J. A. (2004, August). Defining Servant Leadership: A recommended typology for servant leadership studies. In Servant Leadership Research Roundtable. Conference conducted at the School of Leadership Studies, Regent University, Virginia Beach, VA. Retrieved from http://www.regent.edu/acad/global/publications/sl_proc eedings/2004/laub_defining_servant.pdf

Paz, O. (1997). In light of India. New York, NY: Harcourt Brace.

About Paul E. Greasley, Ph.D.

Dr. Greasley enjoyed a long and successful career as an engineering manager working on the design and development of diesel engines, gas turbine engines, and rocket engines. He was well recognized for his servant leadership skills, his ability to influence his circumstances, and his capacity to connect people with essential resources. He worked and lived in several foreign countries including five years in Moscow, Russia as the Resident Engineer for the RD-180 rocket engine development program. He concluded his career as the Engineering Manager for Systems Engineering and Statistics at a large aerospace company. Paul has extensive experience in leading for profit organizations and is on the Board of Directors of a non-profit organization. He is an active volunteer in his community. He is also an experienced big rig truck driver. Paul holds a Ph.D. in Organizational Leadership, is a published author, and has a keen research interest in the diverse personality characteristics of servant leaders. In addition, he is an Adjunct Professor at Palm Beach Atlantic University at the Masters level in the MacArthur School of Leadership. Paul is the founder and president of Timely Leadership Consulting, LLC and can be reached via *www.timelyleadership.com.*

Chapter 5

20 Points for Success as a Leader

By

David S. Maurer
Lieutenant Colonel, USA, Ret.

Leaders at all levels should, and usually do, strive to do what's right, act fairly, reward and punish appropriately, and exercise care when cultivating their own and their employer's reputation. Leaders must also recognize their responsibility to develop the future leaders in their organizations as well as in other organizations as opportunities arise. Our legacy as leaders will be borne in the number and *quality* of the new leaders we develop going forward. As our future leaders begin to make their mark in their own careers, our significance as leaders is both validated and made enduring.

The 20 points contained herein, while not all inclusive, are basic principles we value and expect from all employees in our organization. We also expect these same values of both emerging and seasoned leaders.

The tenets of integrity, accountability, sense of urgency and responsiveness are among those addressed in this chapter – with a fresh spin on their applicability to our success in the workplace and specifically, as a leader. These "20 Points" bring some clarity to the most typical expectations supervisors have of us and we have of those we supervise. I urge you to consider how YOU display these traits and suggest that after a period of introspection, you develop your own leadership philosophy and consider incorporating these (and any others that suit you and your mission area) into that philosophy. The mere identification and publication of your own leadership philosophy won't be enough. The hard part is demonstrating those principles, exhibiting those traits and living up to that philosophy. It will take time and you will likely stumble, fall, and fail at times as a leader – I certainly have, and doing so again is probable, if not inevitable. But we should not let our missteps deter us from striving to be better leaders. Perhaps our failures will serve to highlight our own shortcomings. The better we understand ourselves, the better we will effectively deal with those in our charge.

The following "20 Points" appear in no particular order; other than the first one!

1. Always Act with Integrity and Honesty

This one is non-negotiable. You either have integrity or you don't. You either behave honestly or you don't. As professionals, who represent not only ourselves but also our agency, company, clients and customers – we can settle for nothing less than 100% integrity and honesty in **all** we do and at **all times**. What we allow will become our standard. There is simply never a good reason for behaving any other way – only an excuse.

2. Respond

Actually, I like the word **"respondability."** This is one characteristic that will separate you from the pack. This is a key to any personal success and critical to the success of your organization. When we are responsive to our customer's or client's needs, and the needs of those around us - we become value-added and an indispensable partner. To be responsive means being available, being prepared to carry out a mission on short or no notice and doing so in a positive and professional manner. Others may not always notice when we are responsive but they *absolutely* notice when we are not. Responsiveness and "respondability" also apply to our co-workers in need. Help one another whenever you can, the next one to need help may be you.

3. Anticipate

We have to think like our clients, supervisors, and teammates think and *before* they do, when possible. When we can anticipate their next question or next requirement or anticipate the next turn in the road that they may not have considered, we add value. Think over the horizon. What may happen next and what does anticipating that possibility do to enhance preparation and appropriate reaction? Anticipation is also taking ACTION. When we sense the need for a meeting, briefing, information sharing or presentation developing – prepare a draft for your boss or the client – don't give him or her a blank page – give the boss something to ponder, change and play with. Senior leaders will appreciate your thinking ahead and saving them some work. It is far easier to edit than to create so we are providing a great service when we take the lead and get out in front of requirements, anticipate needs, develop response options and offer actionable recommendations.

4. Follow-up

You may have heard the maxim "an action passed is an action completed." Well, that is *not* the way it works. When you initiate an action – it is YOURS until it is completed. An action that you touch should nag at you until you know it is completed. Don't assume someone else took it over for you – check on it, help move it along and stay on top of it – you are accountable for it – only you. Another aspect of the Follow-Up tenet is to close the loop with the people around you. When you are asked a question, answer it. When someone is clearly expecting to hear from you – be sure they do. Remember how frustrating it is when you have asked your supervisor, client or colleague a question, sought guidance or wanted clarification before moving forward and the lack of response (and evidently interest) was deafening?! Don't be guilty of the same lack of follow-up with those in your world. Answer the voice mail, reply to the email and set up the meeting. Others are likely depending on you; waiting for information you possess, an analysis you can offer, or a decision only you can make.

5. Identify Problems and Solutions

As professionals and leaders, we are expected to develop and offer solutions to problems we encounter and identify. When you become aware of a problem and simply pass it along to your boss or client without offering a course of action or two to address it, your value is limited. Think about the root cause of the problem, what can be enacted now and in the future to overcome, mitigate or avoid the problem and suggest solutions. When you play a role in shortening the time between problem identification and solution – you become regarded as a problem solver; and you become more valuable to the organization. By the way, the more solutions you generate, the more problems will find you – being the go-to person on the team is a mixed blessing and finding someone on YOUR team with such qualities is a gift!

6. Demonstrate Personal Accountability

When you take on an action or are given a responsibility – your leaders will rightfully hold you ACCOUNTABLE for it. There will be times when you will have to depend on others for help, or input, or other support to complete the action, but you must appreciate that regardless of all that – in the end, you are accountable. You can't walk away and point your finger at someone else who failed you – it was yours to do. So, you will need to muster all your personal and professional skills and use them to garner the support you need to be successful. This is often quite a challenge. Help others and they will, in all likelihood, be there for you. In turn, as a leader, when someone responsible to you is struggling to provide you with the results you require, continue to hold that person accountable for the answer. Provide advice and direction, but don't release the subordinate of his or her responsibility and just do it yourself or task someone else. No one wins in that scenario, and no one learns.

7. Work Hard

I guess this should go without saying but here it is anyway. The work we do is not always a pleasure cruise – sometimes it's fun and energizing but sometimes it is just frustrating, mind numbing hard work. Be grateful when you work in an environment where leaders notice hard work and recognize when that extra effort is applied. If you don't work in such a place or for such people – keep looking because happiness and satisfaction will elude you until you do. You can't shy away from hard work – you are compensated for the work you do so always give it 100% effort and you will never be faulted. Remember the wise words of the baseball manager in the movie *A League of Their Own*, "...if it was easy, everyone would do it."

8. Show a Sense of Urgency

We have to maintain a healthy sense of urgency about our work. This not only keeps the interest high and the adrenaline flowing – it demonstrates our level of concern for the mission at hand. Nothing is more painful to watch than an employee "half-stepping" his or her way through the day. Most anyone can spot it in a minute and those who are pumping along tend to resent those who take on work like it was the Ebola Virus. Complete your work as quickly as you can and show everyone that you care about the task. That pep in your step is another discriminator that separates you from everyone else. When you have a mission to accomplish, *just do it*!

9. Foster Personal Discipline

Be professional. Be on time, be prompt for meetings, dress properly, be prepared wherever you go and don't do anything to embarrass yourself, your organization or the people you represent. More and more emphasis is placed on this trait these days, maybe because it seems to be in shorter supply than in the past. Strive to be the kind of person that others will look up to. Set the bar high for yourself and you will never regret the reaction you get from others or the improved results you derive from within. When you demonstrate a high degree of personal discipline, you can expect to see it in those around you too.

10. Lead by Example and Follow Well and Faithfully

You don't have to be in a leadership position to be a leader. The best leaders lead by example. Everyone watches everyone so be sure what you are demonstrating is what you really want to portray – a capable, confident professional who does his or her job to the best of his or her ability – all day, every day. The military has long had an axiom that you are "on parade 24 hours a day." Remember that and act accordingly. Take charge when you must and do so with confidence – don't be surprised when others follow you. They will. Learn how to be a good follower too. Everyone has a boss and our roles as followers can make or break our leaders and affect the overall success of the entire organization. Good followers tend to grow into good leaders because they understand the other side of the equation. Followership is more than taking orders and doing what you are told. It's adhering to norms, being part of the team and encouraging others to join in the undertaking to achieve a mutual and worthwhile goal.

11. Be Loyal in All Directions

Be loyal to your employer, your supervisor, your co-worker and your subordinates. This is one of those traits that will always cut both ways. This is pretty basic but is often absent or situationally dependent. Loyalty means you don't partake in rumor mongering and you don't trash others behind their backs. Professional disagreements are one thing but backstabbing and the like is disloyalty and it cheapens you and those who engage in it. Loyalty does not imply that you should be blinded by it; not at all. Do what's right but be loyal to those that surround you. If you feel that you must go in another direction, be open and candid with your reasons and do so, but guard against being underhanded and slick. This brings us back to the earlier point on integrity. There may be times as a leader when you will be relied upon to deliver bad news to your boss, have a difficult conversation with a co-worker or counsel a subordinate. In fact, I can't recall or imagine a leader who has not encountered each of these challenges multiple times – it is indeed part of the job. Take on these challenges after careful thought, adequate preparation and a developed understanding of the consequences – intended and otherwise. What you can't do as a leader is ignore problems until they go away. They won't, but you probably will.

12. Be Consistent and Clear

It seems that lately, we hear more and more complaints that leaders and managers are unpredictable in their behavior. Happy and positive one day and critical and even cruel the next. Some workers claim these moods change daily or even hourly. Nothing can be more debilitating and disheartening than not knowing what to do because you fear the unknown response or consequence. Solid leaders are consistent and clear. Their employees know what to expect, within a given range, of course. If you are a supervisor and are of the mind that leaving your staff members confused about what to expect from you next is a good thing – think again. This lack of consistency and clarity only harbors mistrust, ill will and fear. It will often cause one more result – poor performance, which will be a problem for both your employee and you. Being inconsistent and unclear is a sign of disrespect for others and they will come to resent you for it.

As a leader, clarity is also required when making a correction or delivering a negative counseling. Be precise in your identification of the problem or issue at hand. Avoid offering what I call the CHECK ENGINE approach to making a correction. Something is clearly wrong but your ambiguous and uncertain approach to the problem only further confuses the subordinate and fuels the spiral of poor performance. Make careful observations, explain the resulting impact on performance and provide clear direction and unambiguous expectations. Better results are more likely to follow.

13. Show Gratitude and Respect for Others

The Golden Rule applies and they don't call it golden for nothing. Do unto others, as you would have them do unto you. Respect one another as individuals and you will be respected in return – it's that simple. Do you know the PLATINUM RULE? Do unto others as they would like to be done unto. The English is probably wrong but you get the idea. This requires some real people skills and the desire to extend yourself. Get to know those in your charge and learn what is important to each of them. It's not a "one size fits all" workplace. I learned many years ago as a soldier that some people respond to a pat on the back and others fare better after a kick in the pants. It is clearly important that you, as the leader, know which technique is appropriate and with whom. Speaking of a pat on the back – this is very different than a pat on the head. The latter can be viewed as condescending and inappropriate as a professional. Be genuine in your praise and recognition for others and you will be more likely to get the results you hoped for. Respect is one of those unusual commodities that you can only receive by giving.

14. Build Teamwork and Collaboration

You are not alone. Don't ever spend time banging your head on the wall because you feel isolated and alone in your work and can't get ahead of it. Find a teammate, co-worker, supervisor – anyone – and ask for the help you need. Usually, the response will be very positive – you may be surprised. It's tempting to feel vulnerable and insufficient if you need to ask for help, but don't allow that to stop you. In the circle of life, you will find yourself on the opposite side of this need sometime. Getting things done together – may be far more efficient than going it alone. Learn to work together towards a solution. Give and take. Very few people can accomplish great things alone – in fact, I am not sure anyone ever has. It does take cooperation and collaboration to succeed, so extend your reach and permit others to reach out to you to foster true success.

15. Promote a Common Purpose

Call it vision if you like. Good leaders recognize that with no visible, achievable or defined target, even well-intended actions are considered random and arbitrary. Leaders help identify the common purpose and unify the team members to move toward that target. They provide the goal and the means to get there. It can be challenging, but a key role of leadership is explaining how all the disparate parts need to work in concert to achieve success. Without the common purpose defined, employees and teams could find themselves working at less than peak efficiency or worse – working against one another. It may also be necessary to repeat this fairly often. It's easy to get caught up in the daily mission requirements and lose sight of that reason for it all – it will be your job as the leader to remind those around you – sometimes even your boss – of the goals being sought and how what you are doing now will bring about the successful accomplishment of those goals.

16. Infuse Passion

We have all heard much said about the benefits of having a passion for your life's work. It is true, you know. Get passionate about what you are doing. Start to appreciate that what you do makes a difference in the lives of real people out there. If you can't feel energetic and enthused and upbeat about spending your day trying to make things better (systems, outcomes, relationships, and so on), then you need to check for a pulse. Working is great and noble and you should be proud of your daily contributions to the cause, whatever it is. So put that pep in your step and smile more – you are making a difference to a lot of people; a lot more than you probably know.

17. Cultivate Your Reputation

You <u>are</u> your reputation. What does yours say about you? Work every day to improve it by doing what is right, taking care of one another and over-extending yourself to your boss, your client, your customers and your co-workers. Do that, and your reputation will speak volumes about you. Keep this in mind...it's not *who's* right, it's *what's* right, that's important.

18. Display a Seriousness of Purpose and a Sense of Humor

Take your job seriously. Work hard at becoming better at it. Study what you need to learn to become proficient and competent. Work is a serious business and others will be depending on you knowing your job. Yes, work is serious but you still need to have fun. Keep your sense of humor at all costs! Use it to diffuse tense situations but be careful to use it appropriately – never to hurt someone else. No matter how hard the day or how long the hours – it could always be worse. We rarely have bleeding and death to contend with so keep things in perspective.

19. Continue to Grow

You are responsible for your development and growth as a person and professionally. Others may be around to help with training, education and job placement when appropriate, but we each need to take responsibility for discovering what we want to be and how we want to get there. You will always be your best career manager. When you stop growing, you die. Be on the lookout for that next opportunity, inside and outside of your organization, and be prepared. The saying that success is when preparation meets opportunity is really a truism. That said, the most important job is the one you currently have, so give it all your concentration and best efforts. Anything less is unacceptable. Don't get caught up spending your workday looking for a better job while turning in a poor performance in the one you now have. Do your best in all you do and opportunities will present themselves.

20. Care for Those in Your Charge

As a leader, nothing is more defining than the way you take care of those in your service. Your employees depend on you to set and enforce high standards, lead by example, and help them succeed. Leaders who care only for themselves or place themselves above the welfare of others are destined for failure, or at the very best, limited success. The author and poet Maya Angelou quote comes to mind: *"I've learned that people will forget what you said, people will forget what you did, but people will never forget how you made them feel."* How do you make those around you feel? Do they feel respected, trusted, valued and cared for? If not, what are you going to do to fix that? The responsibility of leadership is great and it's yours to bear. You must constantly earn the right to be called a leader.

About Dave Maurer

Dave Maurer offers a wealth of experience as both a career military officer and a senior leader within the private sector. In addition to running his own consulting business, his corporate leadership pedigree includes service as an Executive Vice President with GBX Consultants, Inc. in Northern Virginia and VP or Director for several firms in the Washington, D.C. Metro. He has lead Congressionally-mandated global training programs spanning all 50 states and 17 countries and U.S. Territories in support of military training requirements and has served as a program manager overseeing dozens of initiatives targeting improved access to health care for members of the armed forces and their families. In his various leadership capacities, he has supervised thousands of staff members, trainers and soldiers while ensuring quality service and support to all clients and customers.

Dave earned his bachelor's degree in economics from Seton Hall University and his master's degree in management from Central Michigan University. He was commissioned a second lieutenant in the Army's Adjutant General Corps and served in a wide variety of command and staff positions in the United States and overseas throughout his 22-year military career. His service included tours within the intelligence community and the Joint Staff in the Pentagon, and culminated as the Adjutant General for the United States Military Academy at West Point.

He is a certified Project Management Professional (PMP) and a certified trainer through the National Veterans Training Institute. He serves or has served as a board member for several professional organizations and local chapters including the USO of Metropolitan New York City, the Project Management Institute (PMI), the Association of the United States Army, the Military Officers Association of America and the Editorial Advisory Board of G.I. Jobs Magazine.

As a professional speaker, performance consultant, and trainer, Dave offers a variety of relevant topics for diverse groups and organizations. His audiences and clients have included the World Bank, the CIA, the FBI, the U.S. Marshals Service, the Department of Homeland Security, the U.S. Marine Corps, the U.S. Air Force, several PMI chapters, the Performance Institute, and both large and small enterprises in the private sector. He has presented at the National Press Club in Washington, D.C. and has delivered presentations for the Harvard University Kennedy School of Government, the Virginia Tech

Executive MBA Program, and selected faculty members at the U.S. Military Academy at West Point. Dave is a member of the National Speakers Association and co-author of the book *Are You a King or Queen of Conflict in Project Management?* Published in 2008.

You can contact Dave at:
www.DaveMaurerConsulting.com or email at
info@davemaurerconsulting.com

Chapter 6

A History of Leadership

By

Malcolm O. Munro

Why Bother with Leadership History?

Taking a look at the past gives you the benefit of observing the lives, traits, and behaviors of historical leaders and seeing which were most effective, and why. Referring back to the volumes of research allows you to have a statistically valid affirmation of whatever style you choose to adopt. Lastly, knowing where leadership comes from will give you some understanding of my own thoughts on its strong link to organizational behavior.

Where Did It All Begin?

Most scholars believe that leadership was demonstrated from the very beginning. So how long ago was that? We won't get into that debate about whether the earth is thousands of years old or millions of years old, so let's just say it was well before modern conveniences such as the microwave oven or television. In fact, it was probably about the same time an unsuspecting human put his hand into a glowing orange substance and howled in pain from the intense burning sensation.

How do we know this? Well, the easiest way to find out what early man was like is to look at the nearest representations of primitive times that exist today. Believe it or not, primitive people still live in various parts of the world, namely places like New Guinea and the rugged outback of middle Australia. Studying these people provides us with clues on many aspects of early human history and helps anthropologists determine what certain tools and artifacts were used for. If you are skeptical of this method, I challenge you to figure out a better way!

What we learn about leadership from these primitive people is that most of them live in a tribal society with a chief or someone else of significance that reigns as the physical and sometimes spiritual leader. Even nomadic people have somebody who decides when and where to go when the conditions dictate the tribe must move on.

As time progressed, much of man's history began to be recorded, giving us a much clearer picture of who leaders were, what they were like, and what motivated them.

The Bible provides excellent examples of leaders and leadership traits and behaviors in both the Old and New Testaments. Biblical leaders were a diverse group of people, from interesting and sometimes controversial backgrounds.

One of the earliest biblical leaders (a leader based on task and certainly trait) was Moses. I did a two-year stint as a dental clinic manager in the past and even though only about 22 people reported to me, it absolutely wore me out. Think about Moses! Leading thousands of people through the desert for 40 years, eating the same thing day after day for breakfast, lunch and dinner, putting up with whining, fighting, intense weather conditions, scorpions, snakes and still managing to keep his sanity and all the while keeping the Israelites together and moving forward was quite the feat. I believe a part of him breathed a sigh of relief when God sent him up to Mount Nebo and told him he wouldn't be making the rest of the journey across the Jordan River - I know I would have! Other biblical figures demonstrated leadership through positions as priests, judges, kings, prophets, and apostles.

Ancient Egypt thrived under a strong leadership presence. Whether good or bad, the Pharaoh figure was most definitely in charge. In 2300 BC, in the *Instruction of Ptahhotep*, three qualities were attributed to Pharaoh:

"Authoritative utterness is in thy mouth, perception is in thy heart, and thy tongue is the shrine of justice."[xi]

These qualities, a voice of authority, wisdom, and honesty may be one of the earliest examples of the Trait Theories of leadership, which become popular in the twentieth century.

Ancient Chinese literature often refers to leaders and leadership traits as well. Much of the work of Confucius centers on the need for leaders to be good examples. Lao Tzu proclaimed the virtues of a leader being so "hands off" that his followers even doubted his existence. Even today, some of Tzu's work is still being circulated in military leadership training courses.

The concept of *Humanism* surfaced during the time of the Ancient Greeks. This philosophy extolled the virtues of man, including his infinite wisdom and ability to lead. While the Greeks lauded the leadership qualities of their mythological deities, they also, through literature, proclaimed the great leadership heroics of such significant characters as Odysseus, Nestor, and Agamemnon. Greek philosophers included leadership as one of the central factors in running a successful democracy. The quality of wisdom was paramount in a society that lauded the idea of the "philosopher king".

The Roman Empire was known for borrowing many of the Greek ideas, namely their art and system of religious beliefs. They did however place an interesting twist on leadership. Roman emperors were the supreme authority, even requiring worship as deities. Leadership took on the task of unifying this increasingly diverse group of people as each new conquest introduced foreign slaves into the modern society. This obviously proved to be a challenge, but the effort was assisted by proclamations promising death to those who failed to obey.

In *The Parallel Lives*, Plutarch in about AD 100 listed and compared similarities between fifty Greek and Roman leaders. [xii] Latin Authors such as Caesar, Cicero, and Seneca wrote extensively on leadership and administration.[xiii] As the Roman Empire transitioned from a military society into one of intense religious conviction, the central figure of authority transitioned to the Church, namely to the Pope.

For the first time in centuries, the responsibility for leadership rested directly on a religious authority. Even though the supreme authority was attributed to God, the Pope was viewed as the direct representation and in many ways commanded and received the same respect.

This period of time, the Middle Ages, probably solidified the concept of voluntary and unilateral obedience to spiritual authority more than any other. Man was extremely focused on spiritual things and every remnant of that society typifies his struggle to honor and please God, begging at all times for him to be merciful and forgive his pitiful condition. Take a look at many of the paintings and sculptures from that period. Man is usually depicted in the precarious position of reaching up to God, while struggling against the demons that have a firm grip on his feet, pulling him ever closer into their domain. He is never in control of his destiny, forever resigned to the fact that his dependence on God (or his representative) is all that's keeping him from an eternity of damnation.

The Birth of the "Great Man"

The Renaissance began to change this concept. During this time period, many of the ancient Greek philosophies were dusted off and studied. With them came the reintroduction of Humanism. Man was again lifted to new heights, and even though God was still revered, man was no longer living in fear. Every aspect of society changed in response.

Renaissance artists looked to ancient Greek and Roman sculptures for inspiration and they made art more lifelike, extolling the virtues of man. The Ancient Greeks and Romans liked to sculpt naked people. Why was this? It wasn't because they were a perverted society (although in some ways they were). The Ancient Greeks and Romans saw the human body as something beautiful. Perhaps the greatest monument to the enduring spirit and physical presence of man is Michaelangelo's David. At first glance, you may think this is a tribute to the biblical David. But look carefully. What you will find is the often-overlooked detail of his uncircumcised condition. Hebrews were circumcised as a sign of obedience to God. Michaelangelo's David obviously missed his appointment with the Mohel! What this David is then, standing proudly and confidently is a direct representation of humanist, Renaissance man. [xiv]This concept probably contributed to the idea of the "Great Man" which evolved into the leadership standard that prevailed over the next five centuries.

Military, religious, and government leaders exemplified this Great Man concept over the next several centuries. A great military general such as Napoleon motivated hoards of soldiers into a unified lethal force. Religious leaders like Martin Luther and John Calvin united an increasingly dissatisfied group of Roman Catholics under the concept of Protestantism. Kings, brought forth a royal lineage which led nations through some very tumultuous times.

The Age of Enlightenment once again focused on wisdom and knowledge as traits for any Great Man to have. Science was discovering the secrets of the universe, once thought to be only the private property of God. Great explorers were discovering places on earth that nobody dreamed existed. Humanism was once again affirming to man that he indeed was powerful - all the more reason to trust in those Great Men who hold and control their destiny. Although the Great Man concept provided a feeling of safety and comfort, it painted a very bleak picture for anyone other than a select few to ever aspire to positions of leadership.

The "Great Man" Unmasked

As the 19th Century drew to a close, an entire way of life was also ending. Up until this time, people were content to live in a society where craftsmen created and delivered the basic necessities of life. As the population grew however, people began to realize the potential benefit and need for a system of mass production. What developed, with the help of systems and structures such as Frederick Taylor's principle of Scientific Management, was the system of mass production and assembly lines.

By the late 1940's and early 1950's, researchers began to revisit the subject of leadership. Numerous studies were done and the greatest amount of information was documented during this time. I'll summarize the most significant findings by organizing them into three groups: Trait Theories, Behavioral Theories, and Situational Theories.

The Trait Theory

In 1948, Ralph Stogdill embarked his own journey to study leadership. What he found after reviewing every available scientific study and piece of related literature was that leadership was mainly a product of the personal traits a person possessed. He identified and categorized them in the following arrangement:

Capacity	intelligence, alertness, verbal facility, originality, judgment
Achievement	scholarship, knowledge, athletic accomplishments
Responsibility	dependability, initiative, persistence, aggressiveness, self-confidence, desire to excel
Participation	activity, sociability, cooperation, adaptability, humor
Status	socio-economic, position, popularity

In 1974, Stogdill resumed his journey, this time taking into account 163 studies that were published after his own initial findings. What he found was an affirmation that his own theory of traits was indeed valid.

He provided the following trait profile of successful leaders:

"The leader is characterized by a strong drive for responsibility and task completion, vigor and persistence in pursuit of goals, venturesomeness and originality in problem solving, drive to exercise initiative in social situations, self-confidence and sense of personal identity, willingness to accept consequences of decision and action, readiness to absorb interpersonal stress, willingness to tolerate frustration and delay, ability to influence other persons' behavior, and capacity to structure social interactions to the purpose at hand." [xv]

That's a mouthful isn't it? There's no disputing his findings though - they were based on valid studies and really make sense don't they? The only thing that worries me though is that I'm not sure I was born with a lot of those traits. Some can be learned, but those that are personality related might be out of reach for many of us who want to aspire to leadership. Do behaviors have any significance here?

The Behavioral Theory

Stogdill didn't discount the behavioral aspect of leadership. After all, what good are traits if they don't produce meaningful and helpful behaviors? While Stogdill was busy compiling his early findings, other researchers began examining behaviors in great depth. Halpin and Winer, in conjunction with Ohio State University developed an analysis using data collected by studying 89 B-29 Bomber pilots flying combat missions over Korea in 1951. By compiling the data they collected into a complex matrix, they found that leadership behaviors could be grouped into four major factors:

Consideration	Behavior indicative of friendship, mutual trust, respect and warmth
Initiating Structure	Behavior that organizes and defines relationships or roles, and establishes well-defined patterns of organization, channels of communication, and ways of getting jobs done
Production Emphasis	Behavior which makes up a manner of motivating the group to greater activity by emphasizing the mission or job to be don
Sensitivity or Social Awareness	Sensitivity of the leader to, and his awareness of, social interrelationships and pressures inside or outside the group [xvi]

This was just one of many studies done on leader behavior. Bowers and Seashore in conjunction with the University of Michigan considered Halpin and Winer's findings, along with many others and compiled them into what they called the "Four-Factor Theory" which tied the behaviors into organizational effectiveness. These four factors are:

Support	Behavior that enhances someone else's feeling of personal worth and importance
Interaction Facilitation	Behavior that encourages members of the group to develop close, mutually satisfying relationships
Goal Emphasis	Behavior that stimulates an enthusiasm for meeting the group's goal or achieving performance
Work Facilitation	Behavior that helps achieve goal attainment by such activities such as scheduling, coordinating, planning, and providing resources such as tools, materials, and technical knowledge [xvii]

What does all this mean? Basically, you need to do something with these leadership traits in order to be effective. People will respond favorably or unfavorable based on the types of behavior you exhibit. But really, are traits and behaviors enough? What about the particular situation you find yourself in? What if you have to choose between the needs of the organization and the needs of your employees? What behaviors are the ones you need to succeed in each situation?

The Situational Theory

In 1974, Kerr, Schriesheim, Murphy and Stogdill in cooperation with Ohio State University examined two main task objectives: *Consideration* and *Initiating Structure.*

Consideration was the concern for the needs of the employees, while *Initiating Structure* focused on the needs of the business. This was a real dilemma. Whose needs are more important? Which behaviors and traits work best? The researchers identified the following variables as an example of how various situations, and the desired outcomes of these situations dictate the particular behavior that will be most effective:

Pressure	Urgency, task demands, inter-unit stress, physical danger
Task-Related Satisfaction	The amount of job satisfaction employees have
Subordinate Need for Information	The amount of knowledge needed for employees to perform tasks - this of course varied between skilled and non-skilled, white and blue collar etc
Job Level	The variables that come from the many levels in the organizational hierarchy
Subordinate Expectations	What the followers expect from the leader in terms of support and behavior
Congruence of Leadership Styles	Dealing with the various expectations from different supervisors
Subordinate's Organizational Independence	The worker's perception of how vital they are to the organization - in other words, "would the organization self-destruct if I quit?"
Leader Upward Influence	The worker's knowledge of just how powerful and influential their supervisor is in the hierarchy [xviii]

So what are they saying? In short, a leader needs to know how to balance the needs of the organization and the worker and, for his or her own sake, not neglect either one!

A situational approach means the leader needs to carefully consider the needs of the employees AND the requirements of the organization, before choosing a particular behavior to use. In other words, a leader had better know what motivates the worker and realize that workers aren't stupid! They are more than capable of assessing the climate and politics of the organization and will either be productive or rebel based on how favorable or unfavorable the conditions are.

If a leader leans too far to the Consideration side, the employees may love him, but will quickly lynch him if he turns too far to the Initiating Structure side. Conversely, the organization cannot flourish with Consideration alone - the workplace would turn into some kind of encounter group with people chanting and giving each other hugs all day long! With strict adherence to Initiating Structure however, the organization may find itself dealing with apathy and high turnover. What a headache!

Are Leaders Born or Made?

This is another question that seems to torment students and practitioners of leadership. Would you be surprised if I told you that researchers studied this issue too? Fortunately, the dilemma of "born or made" or "nature or nurture" easily lends itself to study. Numerous studies have been conducted and have more or less answered the question. Would you like to know the answer? Well, before I give it to you, let me tell you about two of the most significant studies and their findings.

The University of Minnesota did a study that measured the personality traits of identical twins separated at birth and raised by different families. 11 traits, including two common leadership factors, social potency and harm avoidance, were studied. Social potency is one of the ingredients in making a person forceful and adept at leadership. Harm avoidance, the tendency to steer away from risk or challenging situations is inversely related to leadership. The data showed that in most cases, these traits were demonstrated in both siblings, therefore somehow genetically linked. If this is true, than we can assume that leaders are born, not made.

But there is also evidence that supports the "made leader" theory. In 1988, three researches studied 191 successful executives in order to find out what they found to be the reason for their success. They concluded, after tabulating all the data, that experience was the common element they all shared:

"People who emerge as candidates for executive jobs may come with a lot of givens, but what happens to them

on the job matters. Knowledge of how the business works, ability to work with senior executives, learning to manage governments, handling tense political situations, firing people - these and many others are the lessons of experience, They are taught on the firing line, by demanding assignments, by good and bad bosses, and by mistakes, setbacks and misfortune. Maybe executives are blessed with characteristics that give them the edge in learning these things, but learn them they must." [xix]

So maybe the answer is that each side has pretty good data to back it up and that both are correct. I'm glad to know that leadership is something we can learn. But I think it's important to realize that what some call traits are more personality-oriented and therefore very difficult to try to change or learn.

And Your Point is?

Actually, if you read this book from cover to cover, you'll discover it. The secret to learning leadership and ultimately becoming a leader is three-fold:

1. Know yourself
2. Know your followers
3. Take your followers someplace

Know Yourself

The journey to leadership begins with some self-reflection. Get to know your SELF by taking assessments such as the Myers-Briggs Type Indicator® or something similar. It's only when we start to understand our own desires, motivations, values, strengths, weaknesses, limitations, and goals that we can begin to search those out from those who would follow us.

Know Your Followers

There's no point in thinking you're a leader if you turn around and nobody's following you! Your only hope to become a better leader, after spending time getting to know your SELF, is to get to know your followers!

Take Your Followers Someplace

Now that you know your SELF and have a better understanding of the people that follow you, you'll need to do something with this relationship. There's no point having leadership abilities if you're not willing to step out and go somewhere with it.

But what if you don't have opportunities at work to become a leader? The good news is that life in general is a proving ground for leaders! Opportunities abound, whether in your job, your family, your neighborhood, your church, your school, or even with your SELF. Volunteer for committees, fundraisers, or community help projects. You'll be amazed at how willing people are to hand you the leadership responsibility! Seize the opportunity and make a difference!

One of my favorite movies is Disney's *The Lion King*. In one sequence, Mufasa the king is watching the sunrise from Pride Rock with his son Simba. As they survey the landscape, Mufasa tells Simba that all the territory the light touches is their kingdom. Simba then asks why he can't go to the shadowy place on the other side – after all, if he's king, then he can do whatever he wants. I think Mufasa's poignant reply aptly sums up leadership:

"There's more to being king than just getting your way all the time"

Leadership requires self-reflection, the understanding of the followers, and the ability and drive to take them someplace. It all begins from within. Leadership needs a firm foundation to flourish – starting with a realization of your own personality and preferences. It takes the willingness to look below the surface of people and understanding the roots of their behavior. Leadership then needs a goal to take people to. There is so much power and potential there! Once again, the world is searching desperately for leaders and leadership. Your opportunities to step up and take the lead are all around you!

Don't wait until tomorrow to start your journey!

About Malcolm O. Munro:

Malcolm O. Munro is the President of **Hired Guns Consulting, LLC.** He is a nationally-recognized author, speaker, consultant and coach who works with companies and organizations in all industries nationally and internationally.

You can reach him and his associates at:

www.HiredGunsConsulting.com

Chapter 7

Eleven Things Your Human Resource Partner

Needs You to Know

By

Lisa G. Phillips, SPHR

There are many things your Human Resource (HR) Partner would like business leaders to know about us. Most importantly, that our profession has changed dramatically in the past five years, and so have we.

1.   Strategic:

We are now found in management meetings, acting as internal consultants to organizational managers instead of pushing paper. The paper-pushing paradigm is past. We are now freed up to focus on making our organizations and their employees the best they can be.

In the past we were seen as the people police or the fashion police, eager to nab unsuspecting employees for minor infractions, bent on creating obstructionist, unreasonable workplace rules for the perverse joy of enforcing them on busy people who had better things to do. Many of us have seen how drastically the world of work has changed and know that we can no longer adopt that approach to organizational issues. We've gained a better understanding of the factors impacting profitability and organizational health both inside and outside our organizations.

In a world where employees now come from all walks of life, from different generations, from anywhere in the world, with varying educational levels, and differing expectations, we see the need to be more strategic and engaged in ensuring that our organizations attract and retain the most talented employees. Then we ensure those employees are appropriately trained, integrated into the organization, have the resources they need to do their jobs, understand and support the organizational culture, and remain engaged and productive. We regularly ask ourselves, "What is the biggest issue facing operations, marketing, and finance?" And then we ask, "How can I put HR tools to work to solve that problem?"

## 2.	Diverse Workforce Needs:

With several generations in the workforce at the same time, we grapple with their often-conflicting workplace needs. We sometimes struggle to craft workplace policies that address the needs of employees from different generations and cultures to ensure they are also in alignment with strategic business objectives. All too often, employee needs and business objectives seem to be in conflict with each other, which add other layers of complexity to our work.

Competition for skilled workers is fierce. Our challenge is to ensure that the workplace is adequately staffed while meeting various federal requirements that govern recruiting and retaining domestic and foreign workers. The various laws that govern the recruiting, hiring, training, and retaining such workers are devilishly complex. We ensure our organizations can hire the workers we need so we can participate in the increasingly competitive global marketplace.

We wrestle with the challenges of creating flexible workplace policies that will meet the needs of workers from the Boomer and Traditionalist generations. They want and expect different options than Millennials, Gen Y or Gen X workers because they are at different stages in their lives and careers.

We will see "roughly 10,000 Baby Boomers turn 65 today, and about 10,000 more will cross that threshold every day for the next 19 years," according to the PEW Research Institute[xxi]. We have to develop solutions that allow for the workers behind Boomers to take their places at some future date. True to their "live to work" reputation, "some Baby Boomers are digging in their heels at the workplace as they approach the traditional retirement age of 65. While the average age at which U.S. retirees *say* they retired has risen steadily from 57 to 61 in the past two decades, Boomers -- the youngest of whom will turn 50 this year -- will likely extend it even further. Nearly half (49%) of Boomers still working say they don't expect to retire until they are 66 or older, including one in 10 who predict they will never retire."[2] And when Boomers leave there often is no one to replace them or their knowledge when they walk out the door.

Due to The Great Recession and the subsequent decimation of many Boomer's retirement accounts and home values, many simply don't have enough saved to retire at the traditional retirement age. We are well aware that Millennials, Gen X and Gen Y are anxiously awaiting their turn to progress within our organizations, so we need to develop lateral careers for them until their time comes to enter the ranks of management.

3.   Flexible Workplaces:

In addition to more "traditional" flexible workplace options, some companies are embracing the 24/7/365 connectedness afforded by new communications technologies. These technologies allow workers to be completely untethered from a traditional workplace and schedule, and some adventurous employers are adopting a more radical Results Only Work Environment (ROWE), where the office is no longer the center of the work universe. In a ROWE employees are free to work whenever and wherever they please, as long as they produce agreed-upon results. They are not required to come to the office on any schedule, no standard work hours are set, most meetings are optional, and paid leave is abolished because employees are trusted to independently get the work done and be responsible about how much or how little time they take off. [3] This presents a set of entirely unique challenges for HR professionals, not the least of which is convincing died-in-the-wool traditionalists that the model will work. Research has shown that companies that adopt a ROWE see measureable increases in profitability, and, once employees and managers adjust to the freedom of a ROWE, a greater level of employee engagement. Going to a ROWE involves a significant paradigm shift in how a business is managed, which benefits are offered, and in crafting workplace policies that reflect the new reality of life in a ROWE. A completely new model for performance management must be developed. Performance discussions can now take place in a cube, office, coffee shop, or by conference call, instant message or text message exchange; managers are encouraged to regularly discuss performance with employees; not monthly, quarterly or annually, but continuously. The change is truly "a major shift from the traditional calculation of Time

+ Physical Presence = Results," (otherwise affectionately known as "butts in the chair"), to one where results are the only things that matter.[4]

Another challenge that comes with flexible workplaces and the 24/7/365 capabilities of modern technology is the blurring of the boundaries between work and family time in new, and sometimes disturbing ways. Workers report that they are never "down" or disconnected from their work due to ubiquitous electronic devices. Many work in environments where they are expected to constantly multitask, responding instantly to email, texts, and other communications. They are challenged with the need to keep up with rapidly-changing industries. Coupled with the personal needs of the employees and their families, it is no wonder that more and more workers report being stressed out and unable to focus, which impacts performance. Many return from vacation as much, and sometimes more stressed than they were when they left.

4.   Doomsday Preppers?

Many of us have become our organization's version of a Doomsday Prepper. We have developed a systematic plan for handling potential disasters or emergencies. We've made preparations to keep employees safe and to minimize disruptions to business operations. Like the popular TV show, we plan for our employees to survive terror threats, epidemics, natural disasters, workplace violence, "dirty" bombs, and other dangers. We plan for their safety, shelter, warmth, food, water, first aid, communication and self-defense in an emergency scenario because we've been told not to expect first responders for several days in the case of a severe event. We work with others in the organization to ensure that business and communication systems are protected and will be up to speed quickly in the aftermath of any emergency.

5. Tech Savvy:

HR has rapidly evolved into a more technology-based profession and HR practitioners at all levels have had to quickly become tech-savvy and in control of organizational metrics and data. HR software is no longer purchased merely to improve the efficiency of HR. Today companies buy these systems to help transform their talent strategies and directly improve employee engagement and the ability to hire.[5] We understand this is a fundamental change for our profession and that we need to get on board - fast. Information management leads to better advising and decision-making, and we work hard to apply that knowledge through use of technology and management of organizational information. We master increasingly sophisticated software that allows us to track all aspects of employee and organizational life. We are even more effective when our systems integrate with other systems within the organization. "The availability of data and the fact that much of the data overlaps finance and HR functions is spurring us to collaborate with finance on the strategic planning front."[6] This integration provides us with information that touches all areas of importance to our organizations and enables us to effectively align HR strategy with business strategy. We often make the case for, set up, and utilize complex software such as the Employee Self-Service (ESS) and then provide training for employees to handle tactical tasks previously done by HR. These systems bring accurate, timely information to employees with a few keystrokes. We make sure the information is correct and relevant to employee and organizational needs.

Managers now have responsibility for many functions previously handled by HR (approving pay increases, performance management, authorizing leave, and creating reports), provided through software known as Manager Self Service (MSS). We train managers in the various HR functions for which they are responsible. Legal and employee management problems can arise when organizations don't allow adequate time or resources for appropriate manager training.

We use the recruiting function of our new software to handle voluminous applicants, screen candidates effectively, respond quickly, and select the best candidates without the time-consuming, paper-intensive practices used in the past. We ensure that our recruiting applications are user-friendly, providing pertinent information about our organization's culture, practices, policies, career paths and benefits. We establish and communicate our organization's brand identity by ensuring a dynamic and advanced web portal for candidate use.

The new paradigm for recruiting means no longer only using job boards; we are now using social media, LinkedIn, targeted sourcing, and workforce analysis and have developed an understanding of how to appeal to Traditionalists, Baby Boomers, Millennials, Gen X and Gen Y applicants.

6.   The Darker Side of Technology:

The implications of Bring Your Own Device (BYOD), social media, corporate intellectual property, privacy protection and data security concerns are still evolving; we try to stay one or two steps ahead in this area. We are integrating social media into efforts to communicate more effectively with employees. We know that new technologies emerge rapidly and there are often no legal or business-industry sector guidelines to help navigate potential pitfalls that may arise with untried technology. There is potential for unintended consequences even though a new road is taken with the best of intentions. There is also potential for major gains in workforce competencies that keep us a step ahead of our competition. We know that our organization can wade into the waters of social media with a new strategy or approach, but that the results are far from guaranteed. We know that our employees (and our competitors) are using social media to talk about us, and we have no real control over the messages they are sending. If an individual happens to be a chronically unhappy employee, or a disgruntled customer, the potential for negative implications escalates, especially if something goes viral.

We use rapidly proliferating apps so employees can complete daily tasks and to put data in their hands at the right time, provide training, deliver information, and help them make decisions on the go. These same mobile devices can be a double-edged sword, contributing to employee distraction during the work day, especially when driving and in meetings.

"Because about 75% of organizations have transitioned to ESS and MSS systems, a consequence of this change is that employees often rely on and interact with technology for most HR needs. Over-reliance on technology can mean that personal relationships and interactions between employees and HR are lost."[7]

Concern about employee behavior while "off duty" can also impact the workplace, as employees post information about their personal lives, (and their sometimes dubious after-work activities), on various social media sites. More employers are visiting these sites in an attempt to learn about current or prospective employees, thereby unwittingly opening themselves up to potential lawsuits. Information they learn while trolling social media sites for information can potentially violate someone's privacy, provide information about their protected class, their religion, or their sexual preferences.

7.   We've Learned the Language of Finance:

Many of us saw the writing on the wall years ago and became familiar with the language of finance. We now know our way around balance sheets, income statements, and budget forecasts and better understand our organization's business and financial challenges. We keep a close eye on these tools, and use them as decision points in conjunction with metrics and data surrounding the HR function, to provide relevant information on aligning HR strategy effectively with organizational strategy. We know we need knowledge of key business metrics and measurements for the entire business, not just HR.   We understand business risks and opportunities. We develop strong relationships with colleagues in finance and accounting.

A recent article in Human Resource Executive Online (hreonline.com), stated that according to research from London-based EY:

"High-performing *companies* – those with EBITDA (earnings before interest, taxes, depreciation and amortization) growth in excess of 10 percent over the past 12 months, and that have had a significant increase in performance across both employee engagement and productivity over the past three years, are more likely to have chief HR officers and CFOs who more regularly collaborate. *The* study also found that collaboration was more likely to take place at high-performing organizations that are large and global in scope."[8] The article said, "Eighty percent of CHROs and CFOs polled said their relationship with their counterparts in HR or finance had become more collaborative in the past three years, with 41% describing it as "much more collaborative" and 38 percent as "a little more collaborative. What is driving this greater collaboration? The research points to issues such as talent scarcity and rising labor costs; the elevation of HR within the corporate hierarchy; changes to business strategy, including many affecting both HR and finance; and changes to operating models as companies seek out greater efficiencies."[9]

8.   Business Acumen:

According to The Society for Human Resource Management (SHRM), business acumen is a key competency required of us. The definition of business acumen is, "the ability to understand and apply information to contribute to the organization's strategic plan."[10] We are expected to demonstrate, among other knowledge, "strategic agility, business knowledge, systems thinking, economic awareness, effective administration, knowledge of finance and accounting, knowledge of sales and marketing, knowledge of technology, knowledge of labor markets, knowledge of business operations/logistics, knowledge of government and regulatory guidelines, and HR and organizational metrics/analytics/business indicators."[11]

We work effectively with line managers to understand the business or industry and the challenges it is facing. We regularly read trade journals and publications, subscribe to relevant association newsletters and keep abreast of the always-changing requirements of changing federal and state law. We have learned to talk in business terms. We don't say, "We reduced turnover," but say instead, "We analyzed the factors surrounding high turnover and quantified the costs of that turnover. After applying various fixes, arrived at in conjunction with department managers, we reduced turnover by 28%. That allowed us to bring $475,000 to the bottom line." We understand the need to earn a seat at the table by demonstrating mastery of complex business information and by making relevant recommendations that take into account our organization's internal challenges, external realities and economic conditions. We evaluate the strengths, weaknesses, opportunities, and threats (SWOT) of a business, a plan or some other venture. We help identify the internal and external factors that will either help or hinder a business or individual from reaching a goal, and present them in a logical, easy-to-understand format and then work with colleagues to formulate an action plan.

9. We are Educated:

Many of us have a BS or BA and many more are obtaining an MA or MS in business management, organizational development, or other related disciplines for a more holistic understanding of organizational challenges. We obtain various professional certifications that require rigorous study and preparation, and we regularly stay abreast of the latest developments in our field to earn recertification.

10. We Understand the Compliance Issues (*and they keep us up at night*):

HR risk management requires a thorough understanding of the growing complexity of legal compliance for employers. Various forms of federal and state legislation will continue to be passed, often without adequate guidelines, and HR professionals grapple with their implementation and interpretation. The recently enacted Affordable Care Act is a prime example of this complexity. We keep track of developments in various employment laws and monitor our organizations to keep from running afoul of various regulatory agencies. We know how to avoid costly litigation, work with legal counsel to resolve or fight issues when litigation is unavoidable, and navigate increasingly burdensome and conflicting laws as they are enacted. Lest you think you needn't understand or abide by them, some slap hefty penalties of $1,000 per employee, per violation, per day, which you pay in addition to up-front attorney costs, damages and penalties.

I had first-hand experience with a previous employer when, for nine months, I became embroiled in correcting the errors of a predecessor who either ignored or did not understand various Employee Retirement Income Security Act (ERISA) laws and plan provisions applicable to the 401k Plan. The employer paid over $1.75million to correct errors that occurred over a five-year period on top of hefty accounting and legal fees.

I know of a law firm who neglected to follow the Fair Labor Standards Act (FLSA) requirements governing payment of overtime to their non-exempt employees, who filed a class action lawsuit. (One of their partners was reported to have said when informed of the violation, "So what? We're all attorneys here. Let them sue us.") The employees did sue and the firm was required to pay out over $2.5million in unpaid overtime to incorrectly classified employees denied overtime payments, a direct hit to the bottom line and a very painful hit to partner profits.

Potentially, steep costs exist for the failure of any manager or supervisor to understand and abide by federal employment laws. All management professionals would benefit from a basic understanding of management and employment-related legal issues, the various federal and state employment laws that apply to the manager/employee relationship, and the way those laws affect their interactions with employees.

There are new legal challenges on the horizon. It is conceivable that soon we will grapple with new legislation addressing privacy rights, family rights, disability rights, gay rights, gender identity rights and an increasing number of age-related claims.

11. We are Expert at Employee Relations *(we know how to deal with the "difficult people" that you would rather not engage)*:

Organizations are often at a loss for effective strategies to deal with bullies, troublemakers, and other difficult employees (and managers). Failure to effectively address the problems caused by these individuals leads to lost productivity, conflict, poor performance, frustration, discipline, and termination, and may result in charges of unfair treatment, discrimination or even employment-related lawsuits. We provide support and direction to our internal clients to develop structured performance plans and strategies for handling problem or difficult employees and/or managers. We create and manage compliant and effective documentation, discipline and termination procedures. We provide guidance on terminating difficult employees.

More and more employees enter our workplaces lacking the interpersonal skills, workplace etiquette and emotional intelligence required to contribute effectively. We deal with employees (and managers) who lack a basic understanding of these areas. We deal with inappropriate workplace behavior and we must possess the competency to address issues such as workplace bullying and unethical behaviors or practices, in some instances putting our own careers on the line when we are pitted against powerful managers or organizational structures who refuse to be held accountable.

In the current business climate it is critical for managers to enhance their effectiveness and that of employees by focusing on interactions that create value and promote creativity. Managers must develop their most effective leadership style, one that meshes their personality, the needs of employees and the organizational culture. We provide coaching to managers and supervisors to increase their effectiveness in motivating others. We help them improve awareness of their personal leadership style, and their self-imposed barriers to development or effectiveness. We enable them to lead from their strengths with confidence.

Finally Can We Talk? - CEO and Management Behavior:

You may not be aware of it (in fact we are often sure that you are not), but your behavior sets the tone for the entire organization. We have seen far too many managers, VP's and C-level executives demand outstanding behavior, top performance and personal sacrifice from employees, while in company or department meetings or during performance reviews. We must then deal with the fall-out of employee disillusionment and disengagement when some of you proceed to lie, or cheat, denigrate and demean employees, not follow through on promises or initiatives, or engage in unethical behavior, often while exhibiting spectacular unawareness of the messages you are sending. Your employees are watching YOU to see if you walk the walk and talk the talk, especially nowadays when employee mistrust of employers is at an all-time high due the downsizing and right-sizing both before and after the recession. It doesn't help that CEO salaries are disproportionately higher than the average employee's salary or that many employees haven't had more than a 2% raise in years. The air of the workplace is often thick with general mistrust of organizational leadership, and sometimes this is directly caused by your actions.

HR can't fix employee morale or lack of engagement when leaders engage in poorly handled layoffs, lack respect for staff, or fail to follow organizational policies. Poor management behavior results in employee performance problems, lack of employee engagement, absenteeism, turnover, and a host of other issues that point back directly to you. Please make sure your actions match your words and remember that you can have an overwhelmingly positive effect on your organization by exhibiting behavior that employees can respect and emulate.

In Conclusion:

We want you to recognize us as strategic partners making significant contributions to the bottom line. We are no longer merely costly administrative overhead. We feel your pain. We are well aware that the way HR handles employee relations and organizational matters has a significant impact on employee engagement and productivity. HR is poised to provide valuable information and guidance to management on holistic organizational issues, especially when we have control of HR metrics that directly affect the organization's financial success.

All too often, we see organizational leadership wait until a disgruntled employee files a lawsuit before taking HR issues seriously. We think it is imperative that you embrace education on HR-related issues for yourselves, managers, and supervisors. That way, we will be on the same page when it comes to handling organizational issues and decision-making. After all, we listened to you when you demanded that HR step up to the plate and learn the language of business, technology and finance in order to be relevant. Turnabout is fair play. We are your partners in organizational management.

Finally, make a commitment to finding the right HR professional for your organization. If, after reading this chapter, you realize that your current HR professional isn't up to snuff, tell him or her to get up to speed, and quickly, or find someone who is. Then ensure your organization has a basic understanding of HR issues in general and of the organization's issues in particular, coupled with strong support for the HR professional. Such support includes inviting us to participate in important meetings and communicating with us about organizational initiatives before they are general knowledge.

We have stepped up to the plate to gain the business savvy CEOs have said they want us to have. But only by allowing us access to and involvement in the business side of organizational life will we be empowered to relay tough messages to management about what needs to be done to sustain an organization's competitive advantage.

Chapter 8

Self-Leadership – The Most Important of the Five

Spheres of Leadership

By

Jeremy R. Stinson

WHAT IS LEADERSHIP?

Leadership can be such a nebulous idea to most. If you ask ten people what's their definition of leadership, you are likely to receive ten different answers. And even though you are presented with some of the world's leading authorities on leadership in this book, none of us will be completely congruent with the other's message.

To a lay person, it's probably easier to take the Potter Stewart (Supreme Court Justice known for his characterization of pornography in Jacobellis v. Ohio) approach, they find it "hard to define, but [they] know it when they see it." It is difficult to be flat-out wrong in defining leadership, but more often than not what I observe is people making common mistakes about what leadership is and isn't, for instance; conflating leadership and management. You lead people, you manage time and resources; or attributing leadership to a position held, rather than an action taken; and arguably the most important, and thus most detrimental misconception – that leadership starts outside of one's self.

Regardless of the differing definitions you may find in your studies, or even in this book, the one constant is the integral part that leadership plays in every aspect of your life. In all our endeavors, success and failure hinges on leadership.

There are plenty of definitions for leadership, but the one definition that best distills the essence of leadership and is applicable in almost any imaginable context for leadership is this: *INFLUENCE.* Nothing more, nothing less. In order to lead effectively, you must influence people to follow. Yes, you may have people in an organization structure that are under you in some org chart who are obligated to comply with your direction due to an employment contract, but in order to effectively lead them, you have to influence them. Otherwise, they're only doing it for the money, or the stability, or the… you fill in the blank.

There is only one condition where that definition (influence) doesn't quite fit. It's when you add the prefix "self" to leadership. I'll talk more about that later in this chapter.

But I will say this; self-leadership is absolutely paramount when it comes to leading others. It instills confidence in followers that the leader's capabilities are sufficient enough to follow – if done right, it inspires followers, which takes them past the threshold of obligation. It also lends a level of authenticity. We all have seen the rapid downfall of "leaders" when their actions don't align with their words. When these two things are incongruent, your character gets called into question. John C. Maxwell says that "if a leader's actions and intentions are constantly working against each other, look at his character to find out why." There you will find the inauthenticity, the lack of self-leadership.

FIVE SPHERES OF LEADERSHIP

In two decades of research and practical application of leadership in the military; as a project/program manager in the public and private sectors; executive leadership in the nonprofit sector; and years spent coaching and consulting small businesses, executives and senior staff personnel, I have identified five distinct areas in a given individual's life in which s/he can practice and provide leadership on a daily basis. I've coined these five areas the *"Five Spheres of Leadership"*(not to be confused with Maxwell's *"Five Levels of Leadership"*). These five spheres are such that, everyone from a child on the playground to the elderly in a retirement home will have interactions in at least one of the five daily. In many cases, it's not unlikely that you will be involved with multiple spheres of leadership. The Five Spheres are as follows:

- **Sphere One – Self-leadership**: Self-leadership consists of everything *you* have to do to become an upstanding, contributing member of your family, any organization, society, and the world. It may be as simple as getting out of bed every morning to be where you are needed, for the people who need you – Or – can mean having the courage and discipline to keep the promises you make to yourself, i.e., going to the gym, eating healthy, abstaining from injurious activities. It also means maintaining your integrity, which in itself is a roadmap for self-leadership. Integrity = Doing the right thing even though no one is looking.

- **Sphere Two – Family and Close Friends**: Whether you are the head of your household, or the youngest member in it, you have a responsibility to each member of your unit to do everything mentioned above. In doing so, you set an example that can be helpful to those who are even your leaders. My pre-teen son and daughter are a constant reminder to me of the good that can be done by simply setting the example. They inspire their mom and me on a daily basis to lead ourselves to the best of our ability, and to lead our household just as well. That influence migrates outside the home as well. Close friends take notice of the example and sometimes unknowingly take on some of the same characteristics.

- **Sphere Three – Voluntary Association**: When you volunteer to join a church, rotary club, Toastmasters, you make a conscience choice to pour value into an organization with your time, talents and money. This is altruism at its highest. Leading in this sphere doesn't necessarily mean that you hold a leadership position. It could mean that you influence the organization to do a certain thing or go a certain way. This could be in a good or bad way, your actions in sphere one determine that outcome. This, like sphere two, has to be done in conjunction with other spheres by rule of necessity. If you have a family, they should be given the right to consent to the time and resources that may have to be shared with others.

- **Sphere Four – Formal Organization**: I would consider a "formal organization" to be any organization that you have an obligation to that *is not* a moral one. In most cases, it is your job which you are contractually obligated to. Even if you are not in a leadership position, your actions in sphere one will allow you to be a top performer, or one who just gets by in this sphere.

- **Sphere Five – Observers**: There are some people you will never meet in your life, or even come into direct contact with but they observe your actions from afar. They may know *of* you, but they've only seen you from a distance. They see you move. They see the way you carry yourself. They see how you interact with others. Their impression of you can be a good or bad one, depending on how you have comported yourself in spheres 1-5. You influence these people by showing the good that comes from "good living".

Note: Soon to be released is a program containing in-depth analysis of the Five Spheres of Leadership, as well as methods for identifying opportunities to lead in each sphere in your everyday life. Visit www.JeremyRStinson.com for details.

THE MOST IMPORTANT SPHERE (Self-Leadership)

Definition *of self-leadership: Earlier I mentioned that the definition for self-leadership differed from leadership – here's how. Unlike the leadership described in the remaining four spheres, self-leadership cannot be defined simply with the word influence* *(which is ironic considering that influence is your key to success in leadership). Self-leadership is better characterized by the words <u>discipline</u> and <u>consistency</u>. Influence in reference to self is a case of circular logic. I look at like this – a battery can't charge itself. It requires the introduction of new energy from another source to charge. It is possible to self-motivate, but not self-influence.*

In this chapter I will focus on giving a broad overview of **Sphere One – Self-leadership**, the most important of the five. I've found over the years that the situation I run into most often is that people consider leadership to be something that someone else does, but is out of reach for them. This couldn't be further from the truth.

Famed leadership guru, Ken Blanchard says that "effective leadership is a transformational journey beginning with self-leadership". Author Tim Milburn says that "self-leadership precedes successful leadership". This is not a new idea, self-help gurus and leadership authors like Napoleon Hill, Earl Nightingale, and Zig Ziglar, John C. Maxwell, Stephen Covey, Robert Kelley, and a plethora of others have all written on the importance of leading one's self in order to reap financial gain or simply to become a better person, and yes, a better leader.

In almost all situations where leadership is lacking, it can be traced to not only a dearth of leadership from the top, but also a lack of self-leadership from the members that make-up an organization, be it a Fortune 500 company, or the typical family. Leadership from the top is important for setting vision, but just as important is that an individual accepts the notion that leadership starts within him/herself – Self-leadership. Self-leadership is the fuel that keeps the machine running, in that, members are empowered to fill the gap even if they're not told to do so. They see a problem, they fix it without prodding. When members are self-leaders in an organization, you will rarely hear, "that's not my job".

Another aspect in which we can look at this is from the position of the leadership who has failed to lead himself. The Apostle Paul wrote in 1 Corinthians 9:27, "I discipline my body and keep it under control, lest after preaching to others I myself should be disqualified." It seems like a steady drumbeat of leaders are falling from grace nowadays. They betray the trust of their followers and sabotage the success of their organizations. In his book "Leading From the Inside Out", Samuel Rima states: "The way in which a leader conducts his personal life does, in fact, have a profound impact on his ability to exercise effective public leadership. You must be diligent in the guarding of your character.

Practical Application

It takes discipline and consistency to do what you know is right in a sustained fashion, thus creating good habits. Ancient Chinese philosopher and founder of the religion of Taoism, Lao Tzu (circa 600 B.C.), said "Watch your thoughts; they become words. Watch your words; they become actions. Watch your actions; they become habit. Watch your habits; they become character. Watch your character; it becomes your destiny." King Solomon said in Proverbs 23:7, "As a man thinketh in his heart, so is he". These quotes exhibit self-leadership on a granular level.

So what does this look like in everyday life? Here are two stories in example.

1. I once read a story in a national newspaper about a high school junior who lost both of his parents in a fatal car accident. His girlfriend's parents took him in and allowed the teen to live with them for his senior year, attempting to provide stability at this tumultuous time in his life. Prior to the accident, he was a star athlete and B+ student. Post accident, the young man didn't let the adversity slow him down, in fact, he used it as a catalyst to excel. He put his nose to the grindstone and RAISED his GPA to a 4.0, all while maintaining star athlete status, and applying and

being accepted to several schools on both academic and athletic scholarships.

This young man's story wasn't presented as a case study in self-leadership, although it did a good job at illustrating it. The author focused on making a good situation from a bad one, but didn't go into detail about what is required to sustain one's self after such a horrific event. Yes, he had help, but the discipline, consistency, and courage that it takes to withstand such a devastating loss while keeping focus on what is important at the moment comes from within. I don't know how this kid's life will turn out, but I'd be willing to put my money on him to be a success. At a very young age, he has mastered what most adults have yet to do, well into their professional lives.

2. Early in my military career I struggled with finding my way. I wasn't a troublemaker, but I certainly wasn't a stellar performer. I spent the first year on auto-pilot, just going with the flow and contributing the minimum. In fact, I recall making the following statement with an air of bravado and pride in regards to my work ethic: "I work hard when it's something I want to do". Imagine having to work alongside someone with that attitude. Frankly, I'm embarrassed to recount this incident.

By the end of my second year I had wised up and realized that there was a method to this madness we call the military. I learned the rules – what happens when you learn the rules is you learn how to bend the rules and ultimately play the game by your own rules without provoking the ire of the powers that be. In fact, it was just the opposite – I became the 'Golden Boy". I started crafting myself into the model sailor. I earned 3 ranks in just over a year. My uniforms were immaculate, my boots were spit-shined. I became the top electrician in the battalion, and one of the top five sailors who held the rank of E-5 in the battalion. I was recruited for the sweetest details and assignments. I applied for and was granted access to training designated for ranks above my own. I could do no wrong.

What brought about this change? If I was asked at that time I would have said something like, "in order to make my unit better, I have to make myself better first." Yes, I wanted the training and all of the perks that went along with being "the best", but ultimately, I just wanted to be part of a winning team. If the chain broke, it wouldn't be my link that failed. As a young cocky 20 year old, I couldn't articulate that I felt the need to lead, or influence my unit to greater things, but my actions spoke volumes. I became a high performer. My fire-team became high performers. Most of my squad became high performers. I'm not presumptuous enough to think that I sparked some type of evolution and growth around me single-handedly, but I know there was an example set.

THE TAKEAWAY

What I want you as the reader to glean from this chapter is this:

1. Leadership = Influence
2. Leadership starts with you. The first and most difficult person you ever will have to lead is YOU.
3. You are presented with opportunities to lead in one or more of the five spheres every day of your life.
4. In order to effectively lead anyone else, you have to first master self.

Self-leadership requires discipline, consistency, courage and integrity

[i] The complete survey report is available online using the key words "2009 leadership survey report."

[ii] Read the following to learn more about results-driven leadership: Ulrich, D., Zenger, J., & Smallwood, N. (1999). *Results-Based Leadership: How Leaders Build the Business and Improve the Bottom Line.* Boston, MA. Harvard Business Press

[iii] For information on building leaders' decision-making capability, see Adzeh, J.K. (2013). *Eight-Step Model of Decision-Making: A Practical Guide for Managers and Leaders.* In The Big Book of Management: Tools and Techniques Every Manager Needs in Their Toolbox. (pp 15-38) Main Line Press: Montgomery Village, MD

[iv] See the following for more on the Path-goal theory of leadership. House, J. R. (1996). Path-Goal Theory of Leadership: Lessons, Legacy, and reformulated Theory. *Leadership Quarterly, 7*(3)323-352; Northouse, P. (2013). Leadership Theory and Practice. Thousand Oaks: Sage Publications, Inc.

[v] See the following for more on Steve Jobs' legacy. "Steve Jobs Biography: Inventor (1955–2011)" at http://www.biography.com

[vi] Even though the stories reported in this chapter are true, all names have been changed to protect privacy. Any similarity is pure coincidental.

[vii] Finding Your Own North Star, Claiming the Life You Were Meant to Live, Martha Beck; http://www.amazon.com/Finding-Your-Own-North-Star-ebook/dp/B0019O6IXE/ref=sr_1_1?ie=UTF8&qid=1411032716&sr=8-1&keywords=finding+your+own+north+star+by+martha+beck

[viii] Spalding Education - Home of Scientifically-based Language Arts Instruction; http://www.spalding.org/index.php?tname=home

[ix] Discover Leadership, Mike Jones http://discoverleadership.com/about

[x] The Customer Comes Second: Put Your People First and Watch 'em Kick Butt, Hal Rosenbluth and Diane McFerrin Peters; http://www.amazon.co.uk/exec/obidos/ASIN/0060526564/qid=1043155804/sr=1-1/ref=sr_1_0_1/202-5172509-3048600

[xi] Lichtheim, M. (1973). *Ancient Egyptian Literature. Vol. 1: The Old and Middle Kingdoms.* Los Angeles: University of California Press.

[xii] Plutarch. (1932). *Lives of the noble Grecians and Romans.* New York: Modern Library.

[xiii] Bass, B. (1974). *Bass & Stogdill's Handbook of Leadership: Theory, Research, and Managerial Applications.* New York: The Free Press.

[xiv] Schaeffer, F. *How Should We Then Live? The Rise and Decline of Western Thought and Culture.* (1983). Illinois: Crossway Books.

[xv] Stogdill, R. (1974) *Handbook of Leadership: A Survey of the Literature.* New York: Free Press.

[xvi] Stogdill, R. and Coons, A. (1957) *Leader Behavior: Its Description and Measurement.* Columbus: Ohio State University.

[xvii]Bowers, D and Seashore, S. (1966) Predicting Organizational Effectiveness with a Four-Factor Theory of Leadership.

[xviii] Kerr, S., Schriesheim, C., Murphy, C. and Stogdill, R. (1974) Toward a Contingency Theory of Leadership Based upon the Consideration and Initiating Structure Literature.

[xix] W. McCall, M. Lombardo, and A. Morrison. (1988). *The Lessons of Experience.* Lexington: Lexington Press.

[xx]PEW Research Center. (2010) Baby Boomers Retire. PEW Research Social & Demographic Trends. http://www.pewresearch.org/daily-number/baby-boomers-retire/

1. Harter, J and Agrawal, S., (January 20, 2014), Baby Boomers: Looking at the Largest Generation. Many Baby Boomers Reluctant to Retire: Engaged, financially struggling boomers more likely to work longer. Gallup Economy**.** http://www.gallup.com/poll/166952/baby-boomers-reluctant-retire.aspx

2. Thompson & Ressler, 2013, Manufacturing Company Gains Serious Competitive Edge in a Tough Industry with Results-Only Work Environment: What happens when a traditionally operated, family business has to completely change their organizational practices in order to compete? They call CultureRx to bring them through. Results-Only Work Environment training. http://www.gorowe.com/about/results-case-studies/

3. Ibid.

4. Bersin, J. (2013) 7 Reasons HR Technology is so Hot Today. Forbes Magazine, http://www.forbes.com/sites/joshbersin/2013/05/31/7-reasons-hr-technology-is-so-hot-today/

5. Ibid.

6. Ibid.

7. Shadovitz, D., (2013) A Dynamic Duo: A new study released by EY suggests a connection between CHRO/CFO collaboration and business performance. HRE Online, http://www.hreonline.com

8. Ibid.

9. Society for Human Resource Management (2012). SHRM Elements for HR Success Competency Model.

10. Ibid.

NOTES

NOTES

NOTES